Feathers In My Cap:
EARLY READING Through EXPERIENCE

By Ellen Cromwell

ACROPOLIS BOOKS LTD.
Washington, D.C. 20009

©Copyright 1980 by Ellen Cromwell

All rights reserved. Except for the inclusion of brief quotations in a review, no part of this book may be reproduced or utilized in any form or by any means, electronic or mechanical, including photocopying, recording or by an information storage and retrieval system, without permission in writing from the publisher

ACROPOLIS BOOKS LTD.
Colortone Building, 2400 17th St., N.W.
Washington, D.C. 20009

Printed in the United States of America by
COLORTONE PRESS, Creative Graphics Inc.
Washington, D.C. 20009

Cover photo by William C. Cromwell.
Design by Robert Hickey.
Illustrated by Susan Singer-Arbutina. See pages 11, 23, 26, 27, 53, 60, 67, 172, 173, 174, 175, 176, 177, 178, 179, 180, 181, 182, 183, 184, 185, 186, 187, 188, 189, 190, and 191.
Illustrations also contributed by Allyson Everngam.

Library of Congress Cataloging in Publication Data

Cromwell, Ellen 1937-
 "Feathers in my cap".

 Bibliography: p.
 Includes index
 1. Reading (Primary)—Language experience approach.
 2. Art in education. I. Title.
LB1525.34.C76   372.4'1   80-14498
ISBN 0-87491-296-2

DEDICATION

To

my husband, Bill, who has inspired, believed in, and supported me from the beginning . . .

my three sons, Bill, John, and Peter . . .

my little daughter, Kristen . . .

my loving parents, Alice and Andrew . . .

my mother-in-law, Gladys, who has inspired my life with creative energy and love. . .

the children at the Early Childhood Center, Rockville, Maryland for their artwork.

TABLE OF CONTENTS

Acknowledgments — 9

Foreword — 11

Introduction — 13

1 A Language Experience Approach To Reading — 17
    What is LEA — 18
    Research Validation — 19
    Language Development During the Early Years — 20
    Language Experience in Early Childhood Education — 22
    Art as Communication — 22

2 A Language Experience Model For Early Education — 27
    Description of the Model — 29
    Activities — 49
    Patterns and Resources — 79

3 Language Experience In The Classroom And In The Home — 87
    Establishing a Climate for Language Experience — 88
    Activities in The Classroom — 95
    Activities in The Home — 119

4 Classroom Activities In The Language Arts — 137
Integrating Language Arts in The Classroom — 138
Conclusion — 169

5 Worksheets in Language Experience Activities — 171

Footnotes — 193

Bibliography — 194

Annotated Bibliography for LEA — 197

Film Adaptations — 205

Children's Records — 208

School Supply Companies — 210

Subject Index — 212

Title Index — 214

ACKNOWLEDGMENTS

To my friends and colleagues at the Early Childhood Center, Rockville, Maryland, and especially to Rhoda Ganz, a special friend and exemplary administrator

To the little children who have influenced my life over the years

To faculty members at The American University and The University of Maryland, especially David Dubois, Gunther Eyck, Alexander Gottesman, Michael Katz, Myra Sadker, and the late Donald Thomas

To other educators who have influenced my thinking over the years: Roach Van Allen, Bruno Bettelheim, James B. Conant, John Dewey, Werner Erhard, Paulo Freire, William Glasser, Maxine Greene, John Holt, Margaret Mead, Jean Piaget, Russell Stauffer, and Sylvia Ashton Warner

To Kenneth Edelson at *Children's House* magazine for publishing the basic language experience model used in this program, co-authored by Ellen Cromwell and Nancy Dworkin (fall 1977, volume 9, no. 6)

To Nancy Dworkin, a very "special" educator who was instrumental in shaping this program at its beginning stages

To Sandy Alpert at Acropolis Books Ltd. for her editorial assistance and conscientious, unfailing support

To Herbert Ezrin and Lewis Morse in appreciation for their legal guidance and friendship

To Peter Cromwell who took care of Kristen during long sessions at the typewriter and provided valuable editorial assistance

Thank you . . .

FOREWORD

Reading, in its most basic form, is really an extension of each individual's personal language. Once children are aware of this, they have taken a big step toward learning how to read independently. They make the big step when they move into a reading experience through art and dictation as detailed in *Feathers In My Cap*. The specific guidelines in this book are useful to parents and teachers as they help young children to record their thoughts and feelings through art activities, communicate them through talk, and then read them from text that has been recorded by an adult.

Children who enter into a reading experience through a language experience approach deal with known vocabulary, reconstruct natural syntax, and deal with personal ideas as they generate basic abilities in word recognition for reading. In many instructional settings, these abilities are developed in laborious, time-consuming sessions that have little or no meaning to learners. Failure for some children is anticipated—even expected. But in the program developed in this book, failure is impossible and progress is assured. Children live and learn in a nonthreatening environment that permits them to conceptualize the following:

- What I can think about I can express in several ways, especially through art and talking.
- What I can talk about can be written by someone else, or I can write it by myself.
- What I can write by myself I can read by myself.
- I can learn to read what other people write for me to read because most of the words we use are the same.

As children mature their concepts about what reading really is in the world about them, they come to realize:

- the value of reading in their own lives
- the skills they need to develop to achieve their reading purposes
- the relationship of reading to thinking
- the stimulation that reading can contribute to creative living.

Using a language experience approach, *Feathers In My Cap* presents a program that is exciting and challenging. It assures a positive beginning reading experience for young children.

DR. ROACH VAN ALLEN
*Professor of Elementary Education
the University of Arizona*

INTRODUCTION

The purpose of this book is to introduce teachers and parents to an exciting and challenging language program, *Feathers In My Cap,* which will insure a positive beginning reading experience for young children. The program was developed from the Language Experience Approach (LEA) currently in wide use by educators as a purposeful and creative approach to reading. *Feathers In My Cap: Early Reading Through Experience* is an effective and enjoyable method of teaching reading at the early childhood level. It can be used in nursery schools, day care centers, early primary grades, and the home. The program may be easily adapted for young children with special education needs and to those of gifted potential who require individualized programs that produce feelings of success and satisfaction. *Feathers in My Cap* is a resource text for specialized workshops, child development classes, and college curriculum courses.

ORIGINS

Feathers In My Cap was introduced at the Early Childhood Center, Rockville, Maryland, as a beginning sight reading program for four and five-year-olds. The program uses children's art as a catalyst for producing child-authored stories that children learn to read. Children easily master their own words and thus begin to master the language arts.

Although art has been recognized as an important medium of self-expression in many language experience programs, this program uses art as the *primary* means of self-expression in producing stories. In developing a language experience model suitable for early childhood education, teachers determined that children respond positively when given an opportunity to tell about their drawings. When asked to draw a picture about a group experience, for example, the children became eager participants in the activity. In recreating their impressions in visual form the children often blended reality and fantasy in charming and expressive ways. Just as they love to share most things that are important in their lives, the children wanted to tell a story about their pictures because they wanted to share.

Since the introduction of this model at the Early Childhood Center, reading has become a "sunburst" experience reflecting the colorful imagination and creative energy of the children. Its influence has extended beyond the classroom and into the home. Children are lively learners in the process and most parents are enthusiastic about reinforcing language experience activities. Many children are reading familiar sight words and simple sentences and are experimenting with other facets of language production. Teachers are looking into their own landscapes and discovering a wealth of natural resources that can be used as subjects for language experience projects. By directing these materials toward children's resources, teachers work with children in an atmosphere of mutual sharing and respect. Parents, teachers, and pupils feel the satisfaction of this joyful approach to beginning reading.

DESCRIPTION

Feathers In My Cap describes a language development program that enables young children to discover the joy and satisfaction of early reading through individual and group experiences that utilize natural resources and creative energy. This program introduces a language experience model designed to facilitate the reading process by providing instructional guidelines and activities for classroom and home use. During the four-step sequence, children share in a group experience which stimulates oral communication, draw a picture about their experience, tell a story about their drawing, and, most important, begin to read and understand its language content.

For a young child, a language experience approach to reading can meet cognitive and affective needs that are crucial to early development. Feeling unthreatened and secure in a language experience environment, children will naturally want to discover more about language acquisition and usage. Since each child-author has a personal investment of pride in his/her own story, he/she will begin to bridge the distance between oral and written communication without the stress that frequently accompanies early reading programs. As he/she expands in language facility, the child will develop the confidence requisite to reading proficiency. As the child experiments with the different facets of language production, reading will become a natural part of the growth of communication skills.

"I love the bus ride and my new lunch box."

Chapter 1

A LANGUAGE EXPERIENCE APPROACH TO READING

Since many parents and teachers may be unfamiliar with the language experience method, this section provides an overview of the concept. It provides a sound basis for understanding and applying the model which is designed for early childhood education and described in Chapter 2.

WHAT IS LEA?

The Language Experience Approach has been considered by many educators to be a landmark in reading approaches since it was tested in the Reading Study Project in San Diego County during the 1959-60 school year. A complex concept in theory, LEA may be simply described as "written-down talk" emanating from children's own oral language.

The emphasis on personal language as a primary communication resource is common to all LEA programs.

Since oral language is emphasized as a springboard to language experience activities, children grow in confidence as they grow in language facility. As they bring their own uniqueness to a language experience activity, their thoughts become actualized in original stories. As their stories are read and reread, children begin to master language content without the barriers sometimes associated with the phonic approach.

The essential value of LEA as a reading method is not the number of books that can be created but the process that leads to each creation. The process enables children to develop a secure foundation and feel a great sense of accomplishment.

Since the program has its foundation in the oral and written expression of children and derives its material from this resource, no particular series of books provides uniform instruction and reading objectives for classroom use. Most LEA programs, however, do offer independent work tasks to enhance and expand upon language experience concepts.[1] For example, children may be encouraged to write experience charts, keep picture dictionaries, label key word items, work with word attack skills, study language form, style, and structure, learn to use a dictionary and a library, keep a word bank and maintain a word list. They learn to spell accurately, and to evaluate their own progress.

Moreover, the existing language of children can activate all aspects of language development, achieving a "wanting to" rather than a "having to" attitude toward learning. Although the instructional approaches may vary in scope and content, the learner is always central to the process. Self-emergence and confidence provide gateways to learning. Feeling comfortable and secure in their learning environment, most children are certain to progress.

RESEARCH VALIDATION

LEA facilitates increased proficiency in oral language, providing a sure foundation for the child's acquisition of reading skills. Loban (1963) studied the language growth of 338 kindergarten children to determine the relationship between oral language skills and reading performance. His research demonstrated a high correlation between the two levels of communication in that children with well-developed oral language abilities were able to read earlier and with greater confidence and proficiency.[2]

The effectiveness of LEA as a sound beginning reading program was determined in a study conducted by the U.S. Office of Education (1964). The study compared a language arts approach to beginning reading instruction with a basic reader approach. Although both approaches proved effective methods for teaching reading, the language arts method produced a higher performance in oral reading, word recognition, the mechanics of language, and intelligence.[3]

LEA has also proven effective in motivating children toward reading competency. A study by Pienaar (1975) in the Saskatoon (Canada) public schools concluded that "the children in LEA were found to have gained immeasurably in awareness, assurance, self-reliance, persistence, and cooperativeness. They were eager to express themselves, and they read and wrote fluently and expressively. Every child in both classes had written his or her own reading book and some children had written as many as six books. Their total linguistic performance was impressive, and comfortably exceeded the performance of children in comparable classes elsewhere in the system."[4]

LANGUAGE DEVELOPMENT DURING THE EARLY YEARS

During the early years, language acquisition accompanies natural developmental processes. From earliest babbles to very first words, the young child seems to understand the power of speech. As he interacts with his environment, the child uses language symbols to convey ideas, feelings and interests associated with exploration and human contact. Yet although the young child begins to communicate through oral language at a very early stage, he cannot progress very far without guidance and nourishment. Each step of development holds promise for budding potential and each step must be nourished with love and support.

Given a secure and motivating environment, most young children can begin the reading process during the early years. The four-year-old is capable of comfortably demonstrating reasoning and comprehension skills, particularly if he is given the opportunity to exercise higher levels of thinking. He acquires a sensitivity to word differences and meanings and the basic syntax of language structure. He uses language not only as a social tool but as a natural component of his intellectual development. As he combines thought processes with oral language, he delights in his sense of autonomy and authority. Often this emerging potential will be obscured by the young child's continuing delight in fantasy and fun-oriented activities.

Many children are well on their way to beginning reading experiences by the time they enter kindergarten. Traditionally, this level of development has been viewed as an unfolding stage during which social and emotional needs are emphasized. With the advent of day care centers and preschool training, the emphasis has shifted in recent years toward academic readiness. The impact of educational television, family mobility, and the increasing popularity of recreational and cultural activities have further accelerated early academic trends.

There is, however, a gap between a young child's readiness for advanced learning skills and the availability of sound programs to satisfy these needs. The question is no longer one of "should we," but "how should we," teach reading.

In the search for early reading programs, teachers often introduce materials designed for older children. In many instances these materials are directed to cognitive objectives rather than individual needs. There is a tendency to make the child fit the program irrespective of developmental, social or cultural differences. Children may have imposed upon them static concepts that they cannot understand, let alone master. The results of introducing young children to highly structured or poorly conceptualized reading programs can prove injurious to budding potential and enthusiasm. Alternative methods of teaching reading are needed at the early childhood level.

LANGUAGE EXPERIENCE IN EARLY CHILDHOOD EDUCATION

A language experience approach to reading is considered a natural program for early childhood education for the following reasons:

- It provides a sound and positive foundation for early learning experiences.
- It creates a context for self-development through direct experiences that are familiar and important to the learner.
- It fosters affective and cognitive development by permitting the learner to experience himself while he is discovering important things about learning.
- It permits each learner to progress in his or her own way, at his or her own rate.
- It promotes self-expression experiences as an integral part of the communication process.
- It facilitates a sense of togetherness between adults and children.
- It draws on the existing resources and talents of adults and children.
- It costs little and contributes significantly to early language development.
- It makes reading a meaningful and purposeful experience for young children.

ART AS COMMUNICATION

Most sensitive adults know the importance of children's art as a primary conduit for expressive, uninhibited communication. In his important book, *Language Experiences in Communication,* Roach Van Allen discusses visual portrayal (art) as one of the primary substrands of his theoretical model that explores the growth of language through experiencing, studying, and relating communication.[5] Allen stresses, "self-expression with paints is frequently the most advanced form of communication available to children, with the possible exception of speaking."[6]

Indeed, art can be a central activator and bridge for language experience at the early childhood level. It provides an expressive channel through which children can articulate their thoughts about an experience and sustain their interest through subsequent steps that lead to an original story. In effect, art synthesizes an experience for a child because it enables him to reconstruct the parts of the experience that are meaningful to him. In recreating the original experience through art, the child injects his own perceptions into a new visual expression that derives from, yet expands upon, the original experience.

Victor Lowenfeld describes the process of art as "a dynamic and unifying activity, with a potentially vital role in the education of our children. The process of drawing, painting, or constructing is a complex one in which the child brings together diverse elements of his experience to make a new and meaningful whole. In the process of selecting, interpreting, and reforming these elements, he has given us more than a picture or a sculpture, he has given us a part of himself; how he thinks, how he feels, and how he sees."[7]

Thus, in order for a child to bring meaning to an experience, he must put the experience into some order or structure he can identify with, such as through verbal expression (language) or nonverbal symbolism (art). As the child verbalizes the experience of his own artistic production, he draws on previous understandings and creates a new and original whole. As the child discovers his own paintings or drawings, he will want to verbalize personal impressions in a way that he would not feel free to do in a group setting.

In addition to the cognitive insight art offers to young children, it is a satisfying and rewarding aesthetic experience. Young children enjoy each step involved in painting a picture as much as they do the finished product—the sense of anticipation they feel as the smock is fastened, the satisfaction of picking up and manipulating a paintbrush, the sensory feeling of the brush making contact with a piece of paper, and the excitement of blending and organizing colors. Children may also enjoy the sense of autonomy and control they experience as they stand in front of an easel.

At some point in the child's artistic creation, a form may develop and a theme emerge. When a child leaves the scribbling, formless stage of art and moves into representational forms that are familiar to him, he progresses to a new level of perceptual awareness and conceptualization. The combination of childhood innocence and emerging awareness of reality creates a sense of unparalleled wonder and joy. As the child discovers new ways to express himself, he begins to paint familiar and pleasing objects such as the sun, a house, flowers, family members, pets, and of course, himself.

A young child's paintings fill up space, much as the child fills up his own world. Figures float without linear perspective or direction. Occasionally less common objects, such as prehistoric monsters, space ships, and fantasy creatures, will find their way into children's paintings. Children want to paint what is important or interesting to them at a given moment. As children's art takes on concrete form, they often want to label and verbalize their illustrations. They enjoy the pleasure that others derive from their expressions, but, like any other internalized creation the full meaning is within the experience and the experience is within the child.

"Mother bird and baby bird are flying up to the sun."

FEATHERS IN MY CAP

Chapter 2

A LANGUAGE EXPERIENCE MODEL FOR EARLY EDUCATION

Chapter 2 presents a four-step model designed for early education, examples of group activities that may be used with Step 1 of the model, and patterns and resources that will facilitate understanding and implementation.

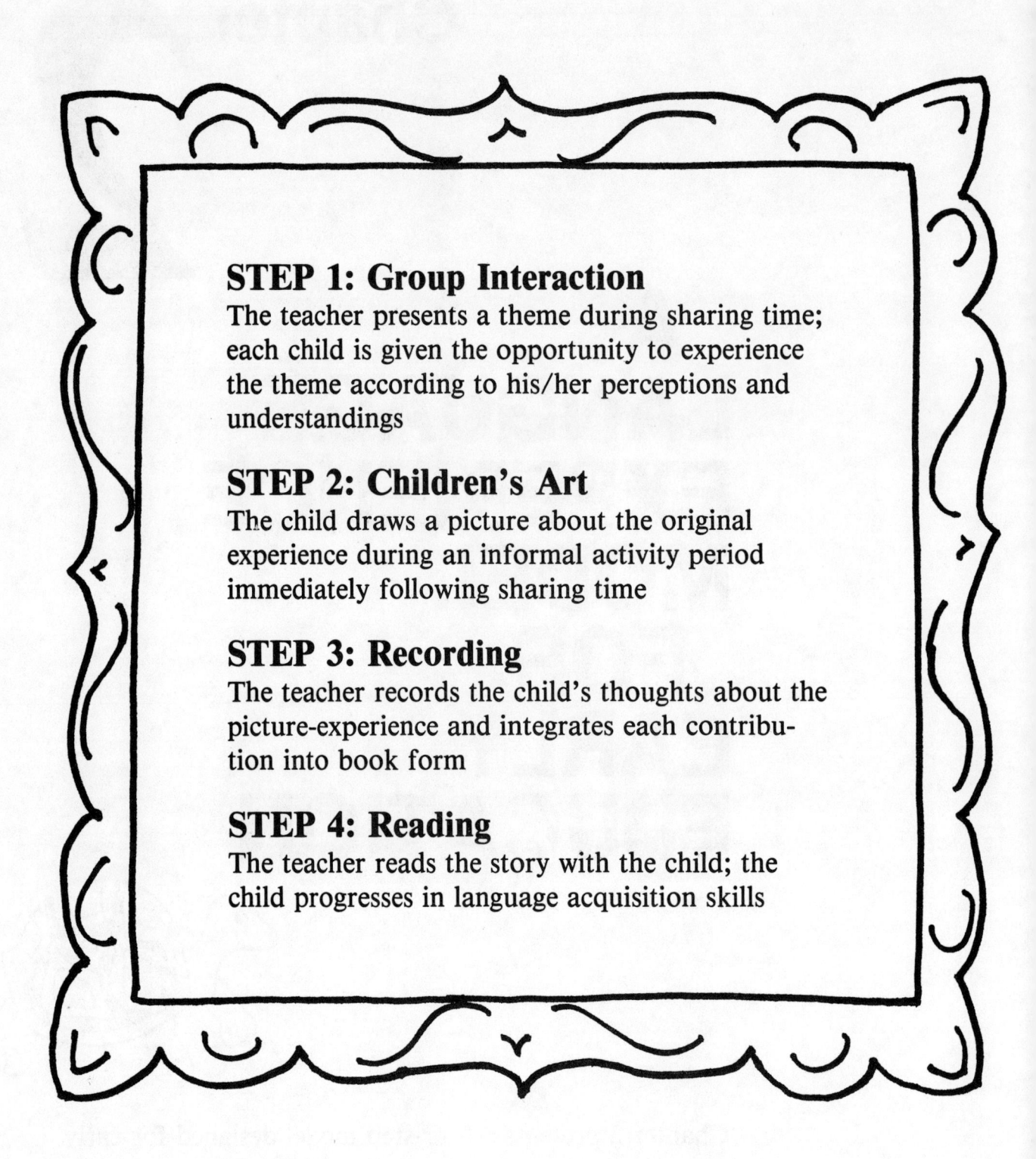

STEP 1: Group Interaction
The teacher presents a theme during sharing time; each child is given the opportunity to experience the theme according to his/her perceptions and understandings

STEP 2: Children's Art
The child draws a picture about the original experience during an informal activity period immediately following sharing time

STEP 3: Recording
The teacher records the child's thoughts about the picture-experience and integrates each contribution into book form

STEP 4: Reading
The teacher reads the story with the child; the child progresses in language acquisition skills

DESCRIPTION OF THE MODEL

STEP 1: Group Interaction

Procedure:
During a structured period of time referred to as "sharing time," the teacher presents an interesting theme to the group to stimulate conversation and creative thinking. Since this period will be followed by free activity, it is recommended that it be scheduled during the early morning hours, preferably shortly after arrival. Such group interaction has particular advantages at the early childhood level. Not only do young children love to participate, but they learn important readiness and social skills as they share and listen to others. Therefore, it is important that the teacher maximize interaction by permitting open, spontaneous dialogue as often as possible.

During this group session, children should be seated on the floor around the teacher. If the room does not have an area rug, children may be seated on individual carpet squares that can be obtained at most carpet stores at little or no expense. Teachers will find that children who have their own carpet space will fidget less and retain more.

Once the children are comfortably seated, the teacher presents her theme, giving opportunities for children to share their impressions voluntarily. The teacher should be ever mindful of the importance of bringing out shy or withdrawn children who may not feel comfortable speaking aloud in the presence of classmates. To maximize group interaction, the teacher should:

- limit a group interaction session to no more than thirty minutes
- encourage children to be good listeners as well as good sharers
- be attentive to children who are insecure in a group setting
- be prepared to digress from a theme if children appear restless or uninterested
- plan a seating arrangement that is comfortable and companionable
- minimize disruptions by removing or covering distracting items
- take care of bathroom and water fountain needs before sharing time
- be flexible, supportive, and animated during group interaction
- select themes that capture imagination, stimulate interest, and bring out personalities.

If the teacher organizes her presentation and directs each theme to the needs and interests of her children, sharing time can become a high point of the day.

Child-Centered Guidelines for Group Interaction: It is important that the teacher consider the personal environment of each child before determining guidelines for group interaction sessions. Even a cursory review of children's records will reveal wide differences in age, maturation, developmental, environmental and experiential backgrounds. In evaluating child-centered needs during group sharing, the teacher must consider such factors as the type of language experience that will motivate a particular group of children, the kinds of behavioral guidelines that will be needed to maintain order and harmony, what problems might preclude open communication, and the responsibilities of teacher assistants during these sessions. Within a child-centered learning environment, teachers should:

- determine how to help children follow directions and acquire comprehension and communication skills
- determine how to help children become active participants in their own learning
- establish personal and group guidelines that are realistic as well as motivational
- use rewards as necessary in order to secure appropriate behavior during group situations
- establish classroom management guidelines that will facilitate order and harmony in any learning context.

At every opportunity, the teacher should allow children to be the source of their own learning. Children should leave sharing time with positive feelings about themselves, their group, and a new learning experience. Using these guidelines, the teacher should be able to set up individual objectives—shaped by each learner and guided by a teacher-friend.

How Often Should Language Experience Themes Be Presented?

It is recommended that teachers present no more than one theme per week for the following reasons:

- Teachers need time to encourage follow-up activities that reinforce and expand on language experience themes.

- Teachers need time to balance language experience projects with other important communication activities such as show and tell, music, unit study, calendar, and weather.

- Children quickly tire from too much of any one thing, even a program as exciting as this one.

How Does the Teacher Select Topics for Sharing Time?

Language experience themes may be presented as special-interest discussions or integrated into a monthly study unit such as transportation, community helpers, self-awareness, modern art, or a seasonal theme. In selecting topics for group interaction the teacher should:

- provide opportunities for children to express themselves through many mediums of communication; for example, puppetry, dance, music, art, cooking, story telling, poetry, films, records, children's literature, field trips

- facilitate concrete understandings by presenting themes with which a young child can identify through observation or association with prior experiences

- plan ahead in order to determine how a theme will be presented and what materials and resources will be needed for the desired outcome

- consider developmental training that may be included in a language experience project, such as attention span, listening skills, following directions, memory, comprehension, divergent thinking, fine/gross motor skills, perception, auditory/visual discrimination, speech development, problem solving, quantitative reasoning

FEATHERS IN MY CAP

- consider attitudinal objectives that may be brought into a language experience project, such as social and emotional development, personality characteristics, interests, fears, home environment factors, health
- consider her own value judgments and biases that might restrict open communication between adult and child
- use visual aids or concrete objects to clarify meanings whenever possible
- call on parents and friends to share a hobby, interest, or occupation with the children
- invite parents or primary guardians to participate in a language experience project in the classroom.

If a theme is carefully selected and implemented through a variety of developmental resources, the children will be eager to make a picture about their impressions of a shared experience (Step 2). For examples of language experience themes, see pages 51-78.

STEP 2: Children's Art

Procedure:
During a free activity period following sharing time, the teacher invites some children to make a picture about a shared experience in a designated language center (see "The Language Center" below). The teacher limits the number of children in the center at any time to approximately six. For example, three children may be drawing picture stories for language experience books, one child may be listening to a record on headphones, and two children may be quietly absorbed in a language activity game in a corner of the center. During Step 2 the teacher should:

- be certain that language experience materials are available in the language center during free activity time
- initiate interest in a drawing project by saying, "Would someone like to make a special picture about (the chosen theme)?"
- keep the center free from noisy distractions and confusion by emphasizing the purpose of the center and the number of children permitted at any one time
- try not to interfere with children while they are drawing a language experience picture
- oversee the number of pictures drawn by each child so that different children may have a turn to contribute to a group story
- praise each contribution even if a child has diverged from the theme (these pictures can go home as daily art projects)
- keep a record of children who have participated in each language experience story.

While some children are busy in the language center, others will be involved in some other activity center such as block play, family life, science or discovery, arts and crafts, or manipulative constructs.[8] In developing activity centers, the teacher must give careful attention to her room arrangement, objectives, materials, and evaluation criteria and the degree of freedom she intends for her children. Although these activities should not require much supervision, the teacher will need to be available for ongoing classroom needs. Since she will need to be in or near the language center when a child appears ready for dictation, it would be helpful if she could delegate some responsibility to an aide or parent helper. If she does not have this support, she may want to introduce a center captain concept, in which appointed children can assist in tying

"I like to read books to my teacher. Did you know I can read?"

A LEA Model

shoes, locating a tissue box, escorting a friend to the bathroom, or initiating pickup at the end of free activity time.

Materials:
A ready supply of newsprint or plain white note paper (recommended size 8½" x 11"), water based markers, and jumbo crayons should be available in the language center at all times. If the teacher plans to reproduce group stories she will need an additional supply of black markers. In addition, small baby food jars (with lids) may be filled with tempera paint for painting sessions. Although markers are favored for detail and ease of handling, sometimes children will want to experiment with paints, especially if they can apply the paint with cotton swabs. Swabs are excellent applicators because they are disposable, easy to manipulate, and tend to "slow down" the young artist, resulting in more detailed art work. If brushes are used for these sessions, teachers should provide thin brushes with small handles. From time to time, the teacher may want to introduce another medium such as watercolors, chalk, or colored pencils.

The Language Center:
Since children spend considerable time in a language center, it is important to understand its concept. This center may be described as a special place devoted to independent discovery and exploration in some facet of learning related to language development. A language center is directed toward independent activities in the language arts, defined traditionally as speaking, reading, writing, and listening. Since art is an important part of this language program, it too must find a place in the language center. (See diagram on page 84.)

The more appealing the center is to a young child, the more time he will spend there. The center should be located away from the mainstream of classroom activity. It may be located in part of a larger room, though children should understand that it is a special place to be kept as free as possible from other classroom activities. The center should give the appearance of a cozy cubicle with a distinct personality. It may be dressed up with an accent rug, a lamp, comfortable cushions, and plants. In addition to accessories, the center should contain a table, several chairs, and a multipurpose storage unit for language projects and activities. The language center should also have sections for listening to records, looking at books, and playing quiet games. An alphabet chart, posters, and pictures that relate to language activities will further increase its usefulness as a communication center. If children feel comfortable, secure, and motivated toward language activities, they will be eager to share with their teacher during Step 3.

STEP 3: Recording

Procedure:
As children become familiar with the language experience process, they will let the teacher know when they are ready for dictation. It is important that children understand the importance of sharing their pictures with the teacher. The teacher may want to refer to children's drawings that are verbalized as "talking pictures." (Similarly, children should be given many opportunities to make "quiet pictures" at the easel—pictures that don't say anything unless the child chooses to give them words.) When a child appears ready for dictation, the teacher should get her pencil and pad, slip into a chair next to the youngster, and "catch" responses before the child loses interest in communicating. The teacher should:

- praise the picture, for example, by saying, "What a beautiful picture; would you like to tell me something about it?"
- record each dictation as accurately as possible
- assign an identical number to the picture and the dictation to facilitate integrating the contributions into book form
- ask the child to print his name under his picture.

Since language experience emphasizes the specialness of children's words, an early childhood program must retain this specialness also. At times, however, a young child will embellish a good thing, necessitating some editing on the part of the teacher. Sometimes it may seem important to retain an entire thought; other times a good thought can be condensed into a simple sentence that would make good early reading material for a young child; and still other times a lengthy sentence can be kept because of the richness and imagination of the language. Long sentences have the advantage of increasing the number of key words (descriptive sight words) that may be used in follow-up activities as primary resources for early reading experiences, (see pp. 139-141).

To encourage full participation in language experience projects, the teacher should keep a checklist of children who have and have not participated in a given month. In time, most of the children will become eager participants, particularly when they see their contributions in a completed book.

Integrating Group Stories:
The teacher is responsible for integrating individual contributions into group stories at an appropriate time in her busy day (usually after school hours). Although the task is not particularly time-consuming, it does require

careful printing in standard upper and lower-case letter form. (see pp. 81, 82).

A flair pen or thin tipped marker may be used for printing.

The teacher should print the child's first name at the bottom of each page containing personal dictation about the picture on the opposite page. If space permits, the teacher may prefer to print (or type) each child's dictation directly under his picture. If she uses this method, she will want to draw a horizontal line several inches from the bottom of each drawing page in order to leave space for children's writing. The size of each picture and the length of dictation will determine the teacher's space needs in coordinating a story. If the teacher plans to reproduce group stories, she should have the children draw pictures in black or red marker so that detail will not be lost in the processing. Children should color in these pictures even though they are reproduced in black and white. The teacher can then add each child's original picture, with the color filled in, to that child's book. When the books have been reproduced and assembled, children will have their own original picture in color and their classmates' pictures to color.

A blank cover page also should be provided. Teachers will probably want to use a lightweight cardboard for this purpose. The cover page will be completed when a title has been selected by the children during Step 4.

STEP 4: Reading

Procedure:

A. READING AND FINDING A TITLE. On the following day, the teacher reads the group story to her children. She should:

- read the story without pausing so that children can grasp the meaning and refresh the experience
- read the story a second time giving children the opportunity to join her; during this reading she points to each word and acknowledges each child author by name
- ask the children whether they would like to assist her in selecting a title, then print the title on the cover of the book and suggest that someone make a cover picture during free activity time.

B. OTHER GROUP ACTIVITIES. The teacher should expand the reading process through the following group activities during the same session, at a later period the same day, or the following day (depending on the size and interest of the group):

- Begin a key word chart (see Chapter 4); print the title of the book at the top center of a large piece of oaktag or construction paper clipped to an easel; number the chart in the upper right-hand corner; assign the book the same number in the upper right-hand corner of the cover page.
- Select descriptive key words from the story and print them in vertical order on the left hand margin of the key word chart; encourage children to help select these words.
- Name each key word as it is printed on the key word chart and identify the letters that make up the word.
- Underline each key word in the corresponding story in order to facilitate recognition and recall in read-back sessions.

- Encourage children to illustrate the key words on the chart during free activity time; the teacher should be prepared to assist with difficult drawings or provide old magazines for this purpose.
- Encourage children to play with key words in the language center; children can practice printing key words and key word sentences until the teacher is able to make activity cards and games to coordinate with each language experience story.

Integrating Early Reading Approaches with Step 4:

A. THE LANGUAGE EXPERIENCE SIGHT WORD APPROACH. Children trained in language experience learn to recognize words by sight (seeing a word in its entirety). Recognition is facilitated by familiarization with words that are taken from language experience stories. A basic premise is that children can distinguish and recall words that are meaningful and a part of their immediate experience. If, for example, a young child is fascinated by balloons, he will remember the word *balloon*.

The main advantages to introducing reading experiences by the sight method are that young children derive instant satisfaction from being able to read whole words; they do not have to struggle with decoding skills; and they do not have to be programmed into a structured instructional approach at the beginning stages of reading when positive feedback is so vital to motivation and competency. When children can identify words by graphic clues or memory, they are getting positive signals about the reading process. (For sight word activities, see Chapter 4.)

B. LETTER RECOGNITION. To further young children's reading experiences, the teacher should familiarize them with the names and shapes of letters in the alphabet. Since naming letters is a favorite activity on children's television, the teacher will probably not have to spend a great deal of time on alphabet practice. Children should be encouraged to practice their letters through simple copywork activities in preparation for independent writing experiences in the language center. A useful way for children to begin these activities is to:

- print each letter in upper and lower-case form on an unlined piece of paper
- outline each letter in a dot-to-dot format and have children trace the letter outline
- have children print their own letters.

C. PHONIC APPROACH. Notwithstanding the facility of young children for whole word recall, it is important to integrate phonics with language experience activities. Understanding the production and combination of sounds that make up words will provide the child additional clues to word identification and strengthen his reading progress. In a phonic approach at the early childhood level, a child is generally taught the beginning sounds of letters and words, vowel and consonant distinctions and blends (two or three consonants whose sounds are blended, e.g., *cl* as in clock). As the child becomes familiar with the sounds of letters, he applies his understandings to combining sounds into words and words into sentences.[9]

An effective way to introduce phonics in a language experience reading program is to:

- set aside one day a week and call it letter day (it should not be on a language experience day)
- ask children to bring a surprise item from home that begins with the letter sound being studied; tell them to conceal the item in a bag; have the child give clues to its identity; classmates have to guess what is in each bag
- plan an activity for each letter sound; for example, on "K" day, write a picture story about a kite, on "S" day, write a picture story about "Sammy the Seal," on "F" day, write a picture story about a special friend, on "A" day, make some applesauce and on "C" day make a carrot cake
- plan a special snack to correspond with each letter friend.

D. INSTANT WORDS. In addition to sight word and phonic experiences, teachers should gradually introduce children to high-frequency words (see page 80). These are common words (e.g., that, was, is, of) that appear over and over in early readers. They are sometimes referred to as instant words. Since these words cannot easily be illustrated, the teacher should use activity games to facilitate retention. She should select words from language experience stories, introducing one instant word at a time. The more instant sight words a child can identify through immediate recall, the faster he will learn to read. A motivating and effective way to teach instant words is by introducing an ongoing "Feathers In My Cap" project (see page 85). Instructions for this activity are:

- Invite children to participate in a magic reading game called "Feathers In My Cap."

FEATHERS IN MY CAP

- Show the children their own caps and explain how each child can fill his cap with feathers: "Twice a week, I will give you a magic feather word printed on one feather. You must take the feather home, sleep on it, return it the next day, and read it aloud. When you have learned the word I will staple each feather to your cap. The more words you learn, the more feathers in your cap! (If you get a magic feather on Friday night, you can sleep on it for two nights, and you will never, ever forget the word!)."

- Keep a magic feather word chart in the classroom and practice instant words as often as possible.

- Send the caps home on special occasions so that children can share their feathers with their families and friends.

- Have the children practice printing magic feather words in the language center.

- Combine the magic feather words with key words from language experience stories and create exciting sentences for children to copy and read.

Children will feel a great sense of achievement as they add feather after feather to their caps!

SUMMARY

The preceding section has defined and illustrated the four steps that can lead young children into early reading experiences. In language experience, the child proceeds from participation in a group activity to illustrating and verbalizing the experience, and finally to early reading activities that relate to an original story. The interaction, illustration, and dictation phases of language experience take place in one period during sharing and free activity time. On the following day, after the teacher has coordinated individual contributions into book form, the children become participants in early reading experiences directed toward recognition of sight words related to group stories.

Perhaps the sequence can best be summarized by the following example:

1. One day, the teacher brings a beautiful sunflower to class for presentation during sharing time. The children experience the flower through sensory sharing and verbalization. The teacher points out the flower's symbolic imagery, size, color, texture, smell, growth processes and useful aspects (the flower contains edible seeds from which oil can be extracted).

2. During free activity time, a child comes to the center and paints a sunflower, emphasizing the face with a happy expression. She paints the stem and leaves last, using whatever space remains to fill up her page.

3. During the recording session, the girl describes her sunflower as her best friend, Wendi:

   "This is a beautiful sunflower named Wendi. She always gives people seeds. One day she gave a seed to a little worm but he didn't like it. I think he spit it out. I wish I had yellow hair like Wendi."

4. The teacher helped the little girl select key words from her story: *sunflower, seeds, worm, yellow,* and *hair*. She learned to read her own story and she never forgot her friend Wendi.

A LEA Model 47

48 FEATHERS IN MY CAP

ACTIVITIES FOR CHAPTER 2:
This section describes two kinds of language experience themes and gives examples of both—themes that may be integrated with an ongoing unit and themes that are contained within a single presentation.

Themes That May Be Integrated with Ongoing Units
An ongoing unit may be described as a teacher-selected subject that contains many subtopics of interest. For example, under the subject "Community Helpers," the teacher may want to acquaint her children with several aspects of community life before completing her unit. In developing her theme, she may plan trips to a firehouse, a supermarket, a railroad station, an airport, and a barbershop as subtopics of interest. If she has scheduled four weeks for her unit, she will probably want to plan four language experience activities, for example, "A Policeman Comes to Class," "My Friend the Mailman," "What I Want to Be When I Grow Up," and "What Do Mommies and Daddies Do All Day?"

FEATHERS IN MY CAP

Example 1

TITLE: **"My Discovery Bag"**

PURPOSE: As part of an ongoing unit entitled "Fall," the teacher hopes to stimulate imagination, acquaint children with the wonders of nature, develop discrimination and sensory skills, encourage creative thinking, and provide incentive for language experience books.

MATERIALS: Paper bags, art materials for decorating "discovery bags," follow-up art project needs such as paste, colored construction paper, brown wrapping paper, magic markers, paints, and crayons.

PROCEDURE: Each child is given a discovery bag to decorate for special items collected on a nature walk. Identifying each treasure by name, the teacher will point out shapes, textures, colors, and smells while children are selecting discovery bag items.

During group interaction in sharing time (Step 1), the teacher will initiate conversation about the nature walk, asking such questions as:
"What was the most interesting thing you found on the walk?
Why do you suppose trees are saying good-bye to their leaf friends this fall?
How would you feel if you were the last leaf on a tree and all your friends had fallen to the ground?
Do you think you would hold on tight all winter long or would you prefer to be with your friends on the ground?
Why are some leaves red and others brown?"

A LEA Model

FOLLOW-UP ACTIVITIES: During free activity time, children are encouraged to draw a picture about the experience for a language experience book. The children may also like to paste some of their treasures on construction paper, sort items by name, shape, and color, or contribute to a classroom mural painted on brown wrapping paper. The teacher may read *Johnny Mapleleaf* by A.R. Tresselt and *A Tree is Nice* by Janice Udry. She may also teach children the following poem (using hand gestures):

Falling Leaves
The red leaves are falling, are falling, are falling,
The red leaves are falling all over the town,
And winter is coming, is coming, is coming,
And winter is coming when the leaves are all down.
Now squirrel is sleeping, is sleeping, is sleeping,
Now squirrel is sleeping curled up in a tree,
And snow falls so gently, so gently, so gently,
And snow falls so gently on you and on me.

Example 2

TITLE:	**"Animal Friends"**
PURPOSE:	As part of an ongoing unit entitled "Fall," the teacher wants to encourage children to care for animals, understand their habitats, ask questions, understand the concept of readiness, and express themselves through language experience picture stories.
MATERIALS:	Visual aids, books about fall, display items on a nature table such as bark, leaves, acorns and pods, a magnifying glass, and art project needs.
PROCEDURE:	During a walk, children observe the activity of squirrels preparing for winter. The teacher should point out the physical characteristics of squirrels, noting how quickly they move from branch to branch, gathering nuts for winter. She may suggest that the children gather acorns for squirrel friends.

When the children have finished gathering nuts, those that are not stored in pockets may be piled underneath a tall tree as "a special gift for our little friends."

A classroom discussion during sharing time may include related questions, such as, "How are your mommies and daddies preparing for winter? Do they have to store food as the squirrels do? Most people no longer have to prepare food for the winter months, but there are still chores to be done—raking leaves, planting bulbs for spring flowers, canning fruits and vegetables

A LEA Model   53

left over from summer, putting up storm windows to conserve energy, cleaning fireplaces, letting down hems from last year's skirts, and looking for a missing mitten!

Pretty soon Mr. Bear will take his long winter's nap—good night, Mr. Bear."

FOLLOW-UP ACTIVITIES: During free activity time, children are encouraged to draw pictures of the experience for language experience books. The teacher may share this poem with her class:

Busy Squirrels
Here is a squirrel with eyes so bright,
Looking for nuts by day and by night.
No time for sleep and no time for play,
She's getting ready for winter today.

Children may want to write their own poem.

"This squirrel is too big for his hole."

FEATHERS IN MY CAP

Example 3

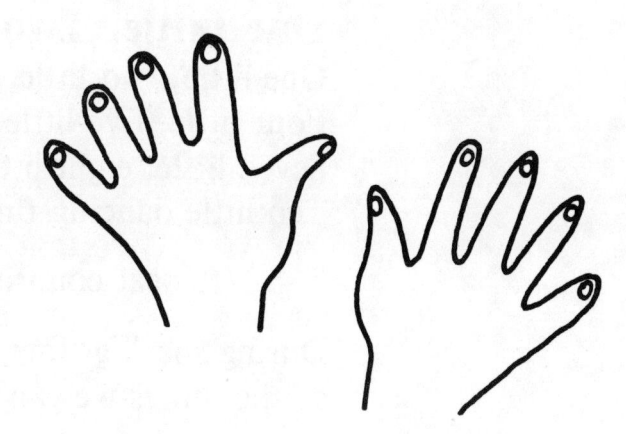

TITLE: **"My Hands"**

PURPOSE: As a part of an ongoing unit entitled "Self-Awareness," the teacher hopes to develop sensory awareness, fine motor skills, perceptual discrimination skills, discovery learning and to encourage children to create a picture story in language experience.

MATERIALS: Items for a "touching bag" might include a magnet, a clothespin, a comb, a spool of thread, a toothbrush, a feather, a piece of cotton, a pencil, a shoelace, a fork, or a hair curler.

PROCEDURE: As a way of introducing one of the five senses, the teacher asks each child to make a handprint on a large piece of construction paper. Directing attention to "our hands," she recites the following finger plays with her group: (authors unknown)

Hands
This is my right hand, I raise it up high.
This is my left hand, I touch the sky.
Right hand, left hand; round, round, round.
Left hand, right hand; pound, pound, pound.

Fingers
Fingers, fingers, everywhere,
Fingers flying through the air,
Fingers making little holes,
Fingers tying little bows,
Fingers learning to button and snap,
Fingers on hands that like to CLAP!

A LEA Model

One Little, Two Little . . .

One little, two little, three little fingers,
Four little, five little, six little fingers,
Seven little, eight little, nine little fingers,
Ten little dancing fingers.

(Repeat counting backward.)

During sharing time, the teacher asks, "What are some of the things we can do with our hands?" Responses may include "catch a ball, eat, tie shoes, brush our teeth, play a drum," and so on. As the children voice such descriptive words, the teacher should print the words on a chalkboard or on a piece of paper. She reviews them with the class before the session is over.

The teacher may play a guessing game with the children, for example, "I'm thinking of something I can do with my hands that makes a loud noise [clap], a soft noise [snap], and no noise at all [wiggles her fingers]." The teacher concludes her group time by introducing children to a "touching bag." Each child reaches into the bag with eyes closed, selects an item, feels it carefully, and tells what it is.

FOLLOW-UP ACTIVITIES: During free activity time, children are encouraged to draw pictures of the experience for a language experience book. Some children may also make a "silly creatures" book. Using the outline of their own hands, they can create a too-tall turkey, a feather happy bird, or a five-tailed duck. Other children may exercise their hands by cleaning one classroom item (e.g., polishing aluminum housekeeping dishes; washing tables, paintbrushes, dolls, and doll clothes; or cleaning their own shoes). The teacher may like to read *Is It Hard, Is It Easy?* by Mary Green.

All kinds of hands!

A LEA Model

FEATHERS IN MY CAP

Example 4

TITLE: **"My Mouth"**

PURPOSE: As part of an ongoing unit entitled "Self-Awareness," the teacher hopes to encourage sound hygiene, good nutrition, sensory awareness, language development, good listening habits, courtesy toward others, and language experience pictures for original books.

MATERIALS: Visual aids that are instructional and informative, such as pictures related to health and nutrition, food categories, and community helpers appropriate to this study unit (e.g., a dietitian, a cook, a dentist, a waitress), and materials for arts and crafts.

PROCEDURE: The teacher begins her unit by introducing the following finger play:

Open Shut Them
Open shut them, open shut them,
Give a little clap,
Open shut them, open shut them,
Lay them in your lap,
Creep them, creep them,
Creep them, creep them,
Right up to your chin,
Open wide your little mouth,
But do not let them in!

(author unknown)

A LEA Model 59

The teacher then asks, "What are some of the things we can do with our mouth?" As the children volunteer such words as *whistle, sing, hum, chew, shout, whisper, open, close, kiss,* and *bite,* the teacher prints the words on a chalkboard and asks the children to read them back.

A visit from a neighborhood dentist will stimulate interest in this theme. He should be asked to bring items with which children are familiar, such as charts, pictures, X-rays, and instruments. He may give each child a piece of dental floss or a toothbrush before leaving.

The visit may be followed by a tasting party consisting of nourishing snacks such as peanut butter on celery sticks, carrots, or fruit. The experience will provide a natural lead-in for language experience pictures.

FOLLOW-UP ACTIVITIES: During free activity time, children are encouraged to draw pictures of the experience for a language experience book. The teacher invites some children to make a "Food That Is Good for Me" book, cutting and pasting food pictures from old magazines. Other children may experiment with mouth fun at the mirror. The teacher suggests that children make a silly mouth, a scary mouth, a sad mouth, a happy mouth. "Now see if you can make your tongue touch your nose. See if you can make it touch your chin!"

Example 5

TITLE: **"Faces"**

PURPOSE: As part of an ongoing unit entitled "Self-Awareness," the teacher hopes to facilitate perceptual discrimination, vocabulary development, sensitivity toward others, and language experience pictures for original books.

MATERIALS: Visual aids that show facial moods and emotions, youthful and mature faces, faces of different colors and characteristics, and materials for arts and crafts.

PROCEDURE: The teacher introduces her theme with the following finger play:

Faces
Two little eyes that open and close,
Two little ears and one little nose,
Two little cheeks and one little chin,
Two little lips with the teeth locked in.

(author unknown)

She may follow this introduction with a special story, such as *Faces* by Barbara Brenner. As the teacher points out the importance and function of eyes, nose, mouth, ears, and hair, she jots down new words on her chalkboard so that children can become familiar with the way these words look in writing. After talking about how faces are alike, the teacher emphasizes how faces are different. She has children feel their faces with their eyes closed. As children are experiencing their faces, the teacher can play the record *Getting to Know Myself* by Hap Palmer.

FOLLOW-UP ACTIVITIES: During free activity time, children are encouraged to draw pictures of the experience for a language experience book. The teacher asks some children to begin a book entitled "All Faces Are Beautiful," in which different kinds of faces can be cut and pasted from magazines or drawn from children's personal experiences and imagination. Another project for children is to fill in a "What Is Missing?" activity sheet on which the teacher has drawn uncompleted parts of a face, for example, a nose with one nostril, an eye without lashes, one ear, and an open mouth without teeth. If time permits, the teacher may read the story *On Mother's Lap* by Ann Scott, or *Annie and the Old One* by Miska Miles.

FEATHERS IN MY CAP

happy faces . . .

A LEA Model

FEATHERS IN MY CAP

ACTIVITIES FOR CHAPTER 2:

Themes That Are Contained Within A Single Presentation

A contained language experience theme may be defined as a specific language activity selected by the teacher for the purpose of writing a group story. Since these presentations not only supply content for stories but create new learning experiences for the children, they should be selected and planned carefully.

66   FEATHERS IN MY CAP

Example 6

TITLE: **"Indian Sand Painting"**

PURPOSE: The teacher wants to develop an appreciation for Indian customs and traditions, an understanding of traditional activities and practices, and a language enrichment opportunity that may be augmented by language experience books related to this theme.

MATERIALS: Powdered tempera paint, sand or corn meal, colored construction paper, glue, paintbrushes, modeling clay, or play dough. (Recipe provided in text.)

PROCEDURE: The teacher reads the book *Tinker and the Medicine Man* by Bernard Wolf. This is the story of a Navajo boy who lives in Monument Valley, Arizona, and wants very much to be a medicine man like his father and grandfather.

A LEA Model

Returning home from a year at school, Tinker observes and participates in all the activities that have been a part of his boyhood. Sand painting is part of a Navajo curing ceremony presided over by a chanting medicine man. A sick person sits on a sand painting that has been made by smoothing ground sand into a flat four-foot circle. In the center of the circle, the medicine man paints a sacred form symbolizing one of the Navajo gods. Tinker is given an enjoyable first lesson in the art of sand painting.

When the teacher has finished reading and discussing this story, she asks the children to help her make a chart of "Words We Know" (e.g., *pottery, weaving, sheep, goat, sand dune, oven, ceremony, sand painting*).

FOLLOW-UP ACTIVITIES: The children are encouraged to make sand paintings for their language experience books. Applying glue with a paintbrush moistened in water, each child paints a picture outline of something he particularly enjoyed about the story. Before the glue dries, each child sprinkles a mixture of one-half powdered paint and one-half corn meal or sand on his picture, shaking off the excess.

As children see their pictures transformed with color, some may want to write a story about their sand paintings. While these children are busy with art work for books, others may experiment with clay or play dough.

A Recipe for Play Dough
3 parts flour
1 part water
1 part salt
food coloring
1 to 2 tablespoons salad oil

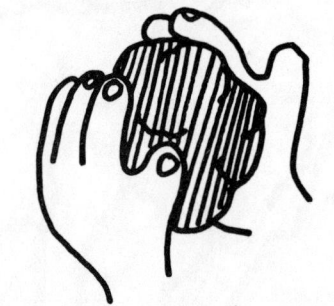

Mix food coloring in water, knead ingredients to desired consistency, adding oil as necessary to moisten and soften mixture.

A LEA Model

"This is Max. He is a turtle. He lives in a creek."

Example 7

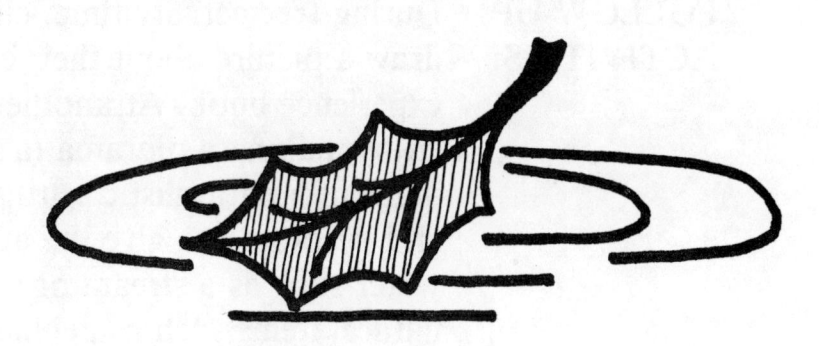

TITLE: "A Nature Walk"

PURPOSE: The teacher would like to encourage an appreciation for nature through direct observation; help children understand cause-effect relationships; develop scientific inquiry through discovery and problem solving experiences; expand visual discrimination skills, memory, and good listening habits; and provide a setting for language experience stories.

MATERIALS: A water table, a sorting tray, shoe boxes, a magnifying glass, and items from nature.

PROCEDURE: For teachers who have access to a park or woodland area, a walk to a pond or stream is one way to provide a firsthand experience for language development. In the process of observing water life, the teacher asks the children: "How does the water look and how does it make you feel? Let's see if we can name all the things our eyes are seeing in the water. Can you see your own reflection? Did you notice that leaf floating on the surface of the water? What would happen if we threw in this tiny stone—would it float or sink?"

On a lucky day, the teacher and her friends may find some tadpoles or other little creatures to observe under a magnifying glass. When children have returned to the classroom, the teacher conducts a brief discussion about the experience while the children are resting.

FOLLOW-UP ACTIVITIES: During free activity time, children are encouraged to draw a picture about their experience for a language experience book. At another table, some children may enjoy making a diorama (a miniature scene depicting items in a naturalistic setting). In a shoe box painted and decorated to give the appearance of a small body of water such as a stream or pond, children can add natural items such as pebbles, sticks, and rocks. They can also make little creatures—tiny fish, a snake, or a frog on a log—from construction paper and clay.

When the diorama is finished, each child can claim possession by posting a sign that says "Marta's Pond" (using the name of the child).

Still other children may entertain themselves in the science center; labeling, sorting, and examining items found. The teacher may add to this experience by reading *Swimmy* by Leo Lionni and *Theodore Turtle* by Ellen MacGregor.

Example 8

TITLE: **"Circus Fun"**

PURPOSE: The teacher wants to generate interest in language experience picture stories; stimulate original thinking and language enrichment; encourage social interaction and self-confidence, stimulate visual imagery and imagination, and create a sense of joy and happiness in the classroom.

MATERIALS: Pictures of circus animals and performers, balloons, materials needed to make simple costumes (e.g., crepe paper, paper plates, yarn, ribbon, and paints).

PROCEDURE: What can be more exciting to children than putting on a circus? The day before the big event can be spent in preparation—decorating the classroom, making costumes, and inviting another class to join the fun (see page 83). Children will want to draw circus people and animals on large 18" x 21" newsprint. (A tailless monkey or a five-legged lion will add to visual delight.)

The teacher and parents can help children with costumes. Some children will have an old Halloween costume to wear, others can make their costumes at school. A paper plate can be transformed into a bear, a dancing dog, or a fierce lion. On opening day (during sharing time), children can march around a center ring made with masking tape. One by one they may come to perform.

FOLLOW-UP ACTIVITIES: Since considerable activity accompanies this theme, children should just be encouraged toward language experience pictures.

"This is me riding a horse in the circus!"

74 FEATHERS IN MY CAP

"I would like to sell balloons that don't pop at the circus."

A LEA Model

FEATHERS IN MY CAP

Example 9

TITLE:	**"Feathered Friends"**
PURPOSE:	The teacher would like to develop understandings about bird life, the concept of migration, the importance of caring for birds, classification and discrimination skills, vocabulary development, creative thinking, and enthusiasm for language experience pictures.
MATERIALS:	Scraps of wood, glue, string, and visual aids.
PROCEDURE:	The teacher begins the group discussion by naming and showing pictures of birds that are common to a given region. The teacher might explain the concept of migration. She may ask the children, "Why do you suppose some birds stay in one place and others travel to warmer climates? What do you think the long trip is like for birds? Why do you think they stay together in a flock? Do you think they will return to their old home when the weather gets warm?" She may invite two children to act out being birds, using "bird talk" chirps instead of real words.
FOLLOW-UP ACTIVITIES:	During free activity time, children are encouraged to draw pictures of the experience for a language experience book. Some children may want to construct a birdhouse with assorted pieces of wood glued together. The house can be personalized with a happy face painted in bright yellow. Children can hang the house on a branch and fill a little tray with bread crumbs or seeds for bird treats.

A LEA Model

Bird mobiles also can be fun. Children can draw, cut out, and paint their favorite birds and hang them on a branch of an indoor tree (place a large branch in a flower pot and fill with dirt) or on a clothes hanger clipped to a window.

The teacher may read the story *Tico and the Golden Wings* by Leo Lionni or *Song of the Swallows* by Leo Politi. The story of Tico could also be told on a flannel board as a subtopic theme for use with a unit on birds. The story is enchantingly real for children, who can easily imagine having their own pair of golden wings like Tico.

"The mommy bird has a worm in her mouth for her baby. She told the dog to get out of her way."

PATTERNS AND RESOURCES FOR CHAPTER 2

The following patterns and resources will prove helpful in developing this program in the classroom and the home.

A LEA Model

Allen List of 100 High-frequency Words in Rank Order[11]

1. the	26. had	51. can	76. how
2. of	27. not	52. out	77. may
3. and	28. or	53. up	78. over
4. a	29. have	54. about	79. made
5. to	30. but	55. so	80. did
6. in	31. one	56. them	81. new
7. is	32. what	57. our	82. after
8. that	33. were	58. into	83. most
9. was	34. an	59. some	84. way
10. he	35. which	60. other	85. down
11. it	36. there	61. then	86. see
12. for	37. we	62. these	87. people
13. as	38. all	63. its	88. any
14. on	39. their	64. than	89. where
15. with	40. she	65. two	90. through
16. his	41. when	66. time	91. me
17. at	42. will	67. could	92. man
18. be	43. said	68. your	93. before
19. are	44. her	69. many	94. back
20. you	45. do	70. like	95. much
21. I	46. has	71. first	96. just
22. this	47. him	72. each	97. little
23. by	48. if	73. only	98. very
24. from	49. no	74. now	99. long
25. they	50. more	75. my	100. good

FEATHERS IN MY CAP

A Letter Chart of Upper- and Lower-Case Letters

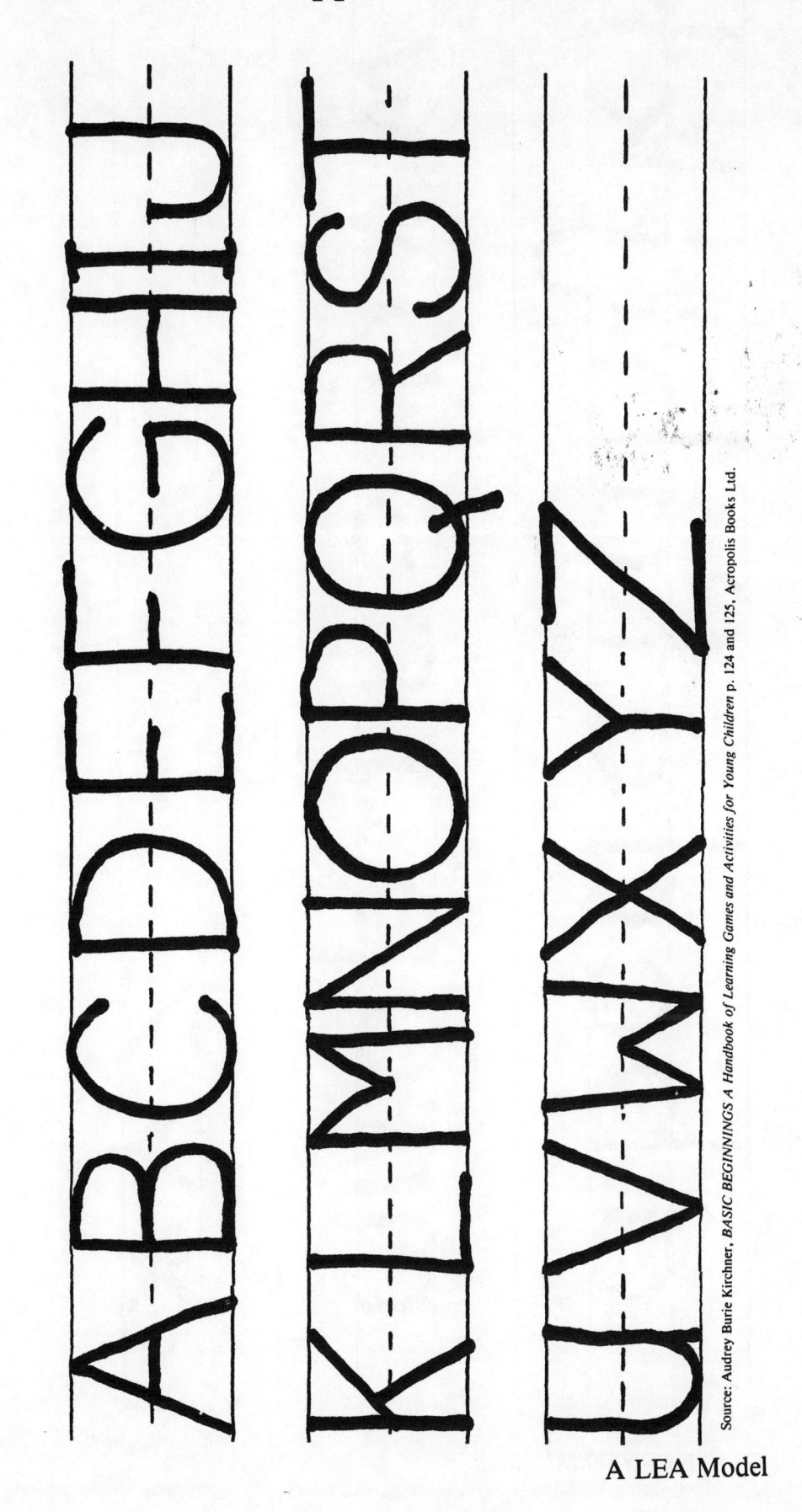

A LEA Model   81

abcdefghijkl
mnopqrstuvw
xyz

Sample of a Language Experience Invitation

An Invitation

To: Mrs. Cutler's Class

From: The Five Year Olds in Mrs. Moody's Class

Date and Time: Wednesday, January 15, at 10:00 A.M.

For: A Special Show: THE CIRCUS!

Postscripts written by each child:

FRED says you will have a great time.

JOSSIE says the lion looks scary but really isn't.

GLORIA says she wishes it could be a real circus.

STEVEN says his lion's mane is making him itch.

MARIA says her grandma is making a costume.

TIMOTHY says he hopes there will be popcorn.

FRANKIE says he doesn't care because he doesn't like popcorn anyway.

KRISTINA says she hopes everyone will behave.

FATIMA says pink is her favorite color and her costume is pink.

MRS. MOODY says she's going to make tickets for everyone!

A LEA Model

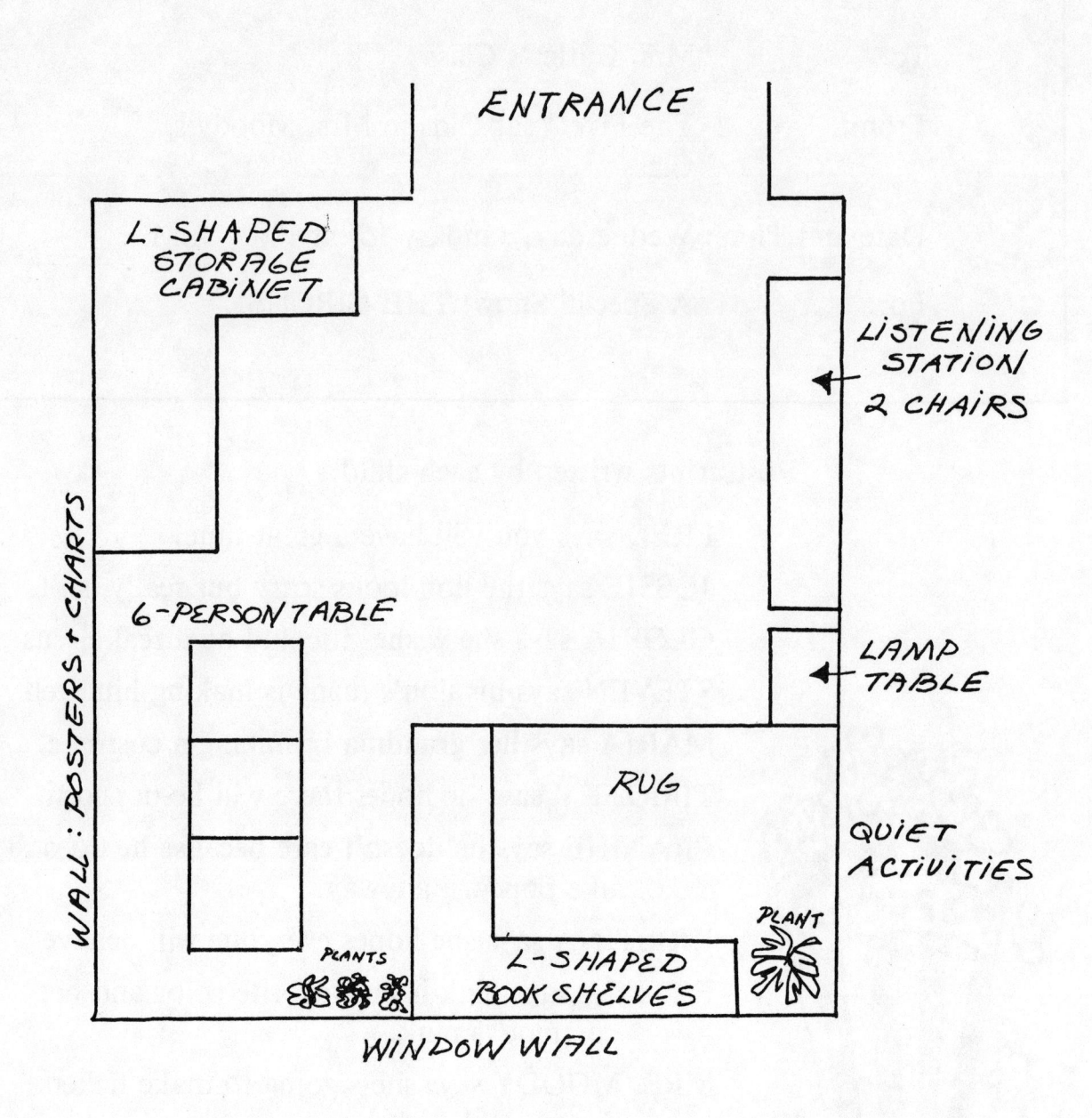

Diagram of a Language Center

Pattern: A "Feathers in my Cap"

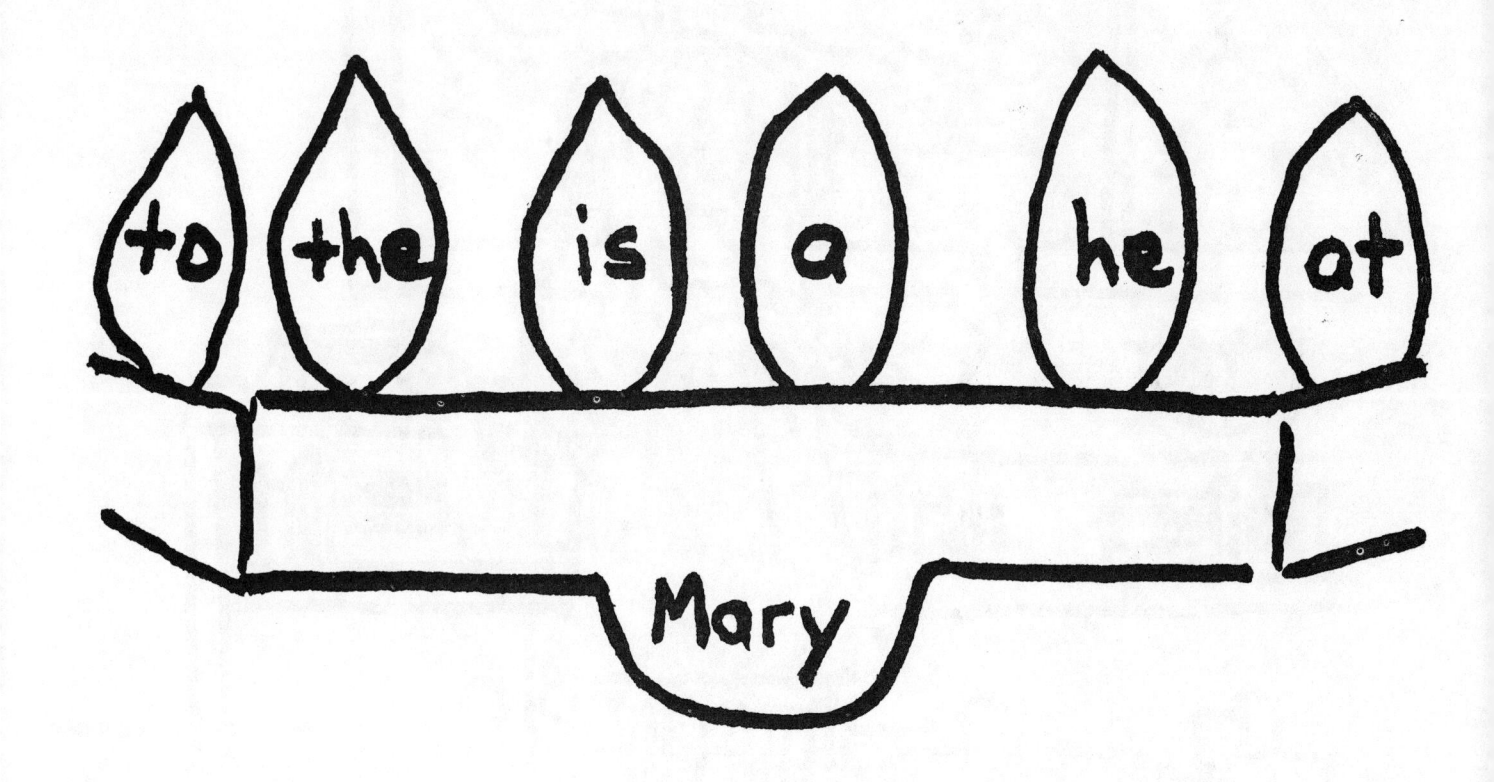

1. Print an instant word on a feather made of colored paper.
2. Staple the feather words to a band made of colored oaktag.
3. Staple on an additional "tail" of oaktag to accommodate extra magic feather words.
4. Print the child's name on the band.

A LEA Model   85

86 FEATHERS IN MY CAP

Chapter 3

LANGUAGE EXPERIENCE IN THE CLASSROOM AND IN THE HOME

Establishing a positive climate for language experience is a major step toward realizing its potential as an early reading program. This section provides an environmental framework for the implementation of a language experience program in school and in the home. It contains themes and illustrations from books actually written by young children.

ESTABLISHING A CLIMATE FOR LANGUAGE EXPERIENCE

The Classroom Environment

Educational programs, like ideas, must germinate. A young child will make contact with a program through his own experiences, instincts, and personal values. If he feels secure about himself and his environment and if he thinks the teacher is a special person, he will sense value in a program and want to work with it. Therefore the psychological environment is the most important feature of a classroom. It is not a consumable item—it cannot be purchased or replaced; it requires no special color or modular arrangement. Although it takes no particular form or shape, the classroom cannot function to its fullest potential without a psychological environment conducive to learning.

Underestimating a young child's capacity for comprehension and need for autonomy, we often impose ideas and values that are ill-suited to the moment. No matter how good a program or how effective a teacher, the child will determine the rate and outcome of his own learning experience. If the teacher accepts the child's need to grasp and internalize each experience, she will be creating a context for success. She understands that the child establishes an attitudinal framework for personal success built on positive experiences and trusting relationships. If the child is accepted for what he is rather than for what he will become, the seeds of growth will germinate.

Once a positive psychological environment has been established in a classroom, the teacher must direct her attention to the purpose and objectives of the program components. If her orientation is humanistic, she will probably feel comfortable with an informal classroom, one that permits a reasonable degree of free choice, autonomy, and open communication. Her choice of programs, manner of presentation, and evaluation criteria will reflect this orientation. She will be receptive to change because she understands that learning is never static and that she, too, must be a part of the growth process. Consequently, she will follow the path of child-centered learning. Her classroom will have centers of interest designed for exploration and discovery. She will not impose limits on her children, yet she will establish boundaries based on realistic expectations that children can understand. She will help children make wise decisions and understand consequences. She will encourage self-direction and cooperation. She will help children recognize the importance of doing everything well, from putting blocks away in their proper place, to washing a table, to being responsible for their own belongings.

The Role of the Teacher

The teacher is the primary model in a preschool classroom. Children look to her for comfort, security and love. The child will accept discipline if it is accompanied by respect, anger if accompanied by love, friendship if accompanied by trust. All things are possible if the teacher extends herself to the learner; if she will, in effect, be both learner and teacher. Children understand qualities of kindness and forgiveness. They read body language before they read words. They look for signals that tell them everything is right in their world.

In language experience activities, the teacher functions as a facilitator and friend. In order to present a theme effectively, she must take time to research and develop the theme, plan objectives, determine activity needs, and collect materials useful for classroom implementation.

During Step 1 of language experience (Group Interaction), the teacher should respect each child as an individual, acknowledge personal contributions, avoid controlling or talking down to children, and equalize interactions so that each child has a chance for self-expression. The teacher should sift through all the conversation, extracting and emphasizing important points. By gesture and voice intonation she conveys a sense of enthusiasm for the subject and the ensuing conversation. Sensitive to signals of fatigue or restlessness, she singles out children in special ways to bring them back to the discussion. She is open to all voices but ever mindful of the need to steer in the direction of her theme.

During Step 2 (Children's Art) and Step 3 (Recording), the teacher is a less conspicuous facilitator as creative energy shifts to the children. Maintaining a positive and cheerful attitude, she encourages children toward the language center so that they will feel motivated to draw a picture about their experience. When a child has finished a picture, the teacher is ready to record dictation by the child without much comment except to personalize the interaction. As a way of monitoring progress, she finds ways to bring less enthusiastic children into the language center. Perhaps, for example, she plays key word card games with children who initially prefer not to draw.

During Step 4 (Reading), the teacher reads the completed story with a pleasant and interesting voice, encouraging children to join her in reading their own words. During language activities in the language center, children look to the teacher for guidance and reinforcement because they cannot always manage their time efficiently and they may lack the skills to work independently. Teachers should encourage children to help each other by explaining the importance of contributing to one another's learning. In an alliance or partnership, the teacher relaxes and enjoys her own experiences with each child.

"My teacher likes to show her teeth when she smiles. I have two new pony tails."

The Home Environment

Parents should be encouraged to become eager participants in language experience, too, and they can stimulate inquiry and incentive in their young children. A trip to the park, the post office, a train terminal, an art gallery, a farm or an orchard can take on special meaning for parent and child and become a subject for language experience stories. If a teacher holds a brief workshop to acquaint parents with this method, the parent will be better able to reinforce a child's sight-reading program in the home. If the parent is acquainted with the program only through papers that come home with the child, he/she should ask the teacher for a few minutes to explain the approach. The parent may also request a copy of a group story or a list of key words for home review. If a child is not being exposed to a language experience program in school and the parent wishes to begin one in the home, he/she will find out how creative and effective the program is. Sharing a language experience project with a child can only strengthen communication between parent and child.

Finding a place for language experience projects in the home need not be complicated or costly. Parents can help children find their own little cozy corner for picture stories. For example, the kitchen table or a section of the dining room, family room, or bedroom. Language experience stories can be kept in a three-ring binder. A large supply of plain white paper and markers will complete the material needs. Young children will love having a book of their own like their big brothers and sisters. Each picture story and key word chart can have its own section in the notebook. The notebook may be entitled "My Picture Story Book" and decorated with little novelties that please young children. Some children will want to write stories about each key word. Most children will want to share their books with family and friends.

"I love Mommy and Daddy because I do."

FEATHERS IN MY CAP

ACTIVITIES FOR CHAPTER 3:

Language Experience in the Classroom

The following themes and picture stories were developed, illustrated, and written at The Early Childhood Center, Rockville, Maryland, employing the model presented in Chapter II.

LEA In Classroom And Home

"My sister got two balloons at the zoo. Isn't she pretty?"

"I wish I could go up in the air like a balloon!"

FEATHERS IN MY CAP

Theme 1

TITLE: **"Balloons"**

PURPOSE: The teacher wished to create a sense of poetic fantasy during a group experience. She wanted to find a way to bring shy children into the group through nonverbal interaction, (such as dance) and she wanted all of her children to experience freedom of movement through an imaginary flight into space. She wanted the experience to include listening for appreciation and understanding through dance and music.

MATERIALS: A red balloon, record player, and an appropriate record.

PROCEDURE: The teacher wrote a story about balloon friends taking a long journey into space. She recorded the story in advance so that she would not need to be the center of attention during the actual presentation. She chose a large red balloon as a focal point in the classroom, creating a sense of wonder in physical form that each child could identify with. She selected Strauss' "Tales From the Vienna Woods" as a musical accompaniment to the children's balloon dance.

When the children gathered for sharing time, the teacher asked them to take off their shoes in preparation for a trip into space. She said:

"Look around boys and girls, we have a new friend in class today. She is round and red, and she can fly! Would you like to join her in space—she doesn't like to fly alone. Before we begin our trip, however, our balloon friend would like us to listen to her story."

LEA In Classroom And Home

The teacher turned on the tape recorder and proceeded with the following dance-story:

"Oh wouldn't it be fun to be a balloon for just a little while; to pick a favorite color, curl up tight and slowly move through space. Would you like to be a balloon? Just close your eyes and imagine yourself a balloon. Gradually unfold; open your arms and expand your bodies out into space. You may sway back and forth at first until you gain confidence and then you will move as though the whole world belongs to you. The gentle wind will be your friend and she will guide you through your long journey. Do not be concerned if you feel soft raindrops fall on you. Slow down and greet the drops. If you tire, rest for awhile on a soft white cloud. Perhaps you will pass a balloon friend when you next resume your flight; just nod and say hello to your traveling companion. Close your eyes and imagine you are looking at haystacks, hills and mountains, grazing cattle, rushing streams and sleepy old houses; flashing lights, bustling cities, and the organ-grinder man! Fly high, my friends, until you are at your journey's end. Then fall gently back to earth and be with your friends—red and yellow, blue and green, deep purple, and silver—beautiful balloons!"

The teacher turned on the music and the children began their dance, moved by the spirit and magic of the moment.

FOLLOW-UP ACTIVITIES: During free activity time some of the children drew pictures about their shared experience in the language center. They chose words to describe their pictures as noted under each illustration.

To further develop this theme, the teacher invited some children to make a balloon mural. She made a word list of objects that were cited in her narration; *raindrops, wind, cloud, balloons, haystack, mountains.* Each child selected one word from this list and painted his impressions of that word on the mural.

On the following day the teacher surprised the children with a jar of bubble soap. As children blew bubbles into the air, they observed movement, shape, and soft colors. The teacher asked the children to compare bubbles and balloons, how are they alike, how are they different, which would you rather be, and why?

"This balloon is flying upside down."

"This balloon doesn't know how to fly. She is a baby balloon."

"This is Mary going up in the air with her balloon."

Theme 2

TITLE: **"Big and Small"**

PURPOSE: The purpose of this experience was to assist young children in understanding beginning concepts of dimension using the following size relationship categories:

    big, small   biggest, smallest
    big, bigger, biggest   small, smaller, smallest

MATERIALS: Wooden blocks in a variety of sizes and a chalkboard.

PROCEDURE: The teacher introduced her theme by asking children for examples of things that are "big" and things that are "small."

    Responses included: mountains, space ships, God, the sky, an elephant, a mouse, an ant, a fly, and stones.

    Using a variety of wooden blocks to demonstrate the concept of size discrimination, the teacher grouped the blocks on a table to correspond with the four categories she had introduced. She used two blocks for group 1 (big, small), several blocks for group 2 (biggest, smallest), three blocks for group 3 (big, bigger, biggest), and three blocks for group 4 (small, smaller, smallest). She labeled these Set 1, Set 2, Set 3, and Set 4, explaining that a set is a collection or group of objects. Each child was asked to point to a size category in one of the sets and to identify the blocks by size.

Drawing three ice cream cones of single, double and triple proportions on a chalkboard, the teacher asked her children, "Which ice cream cone would you prefer, the big, the bigger or the biggest one?" Then she said, "Suppose you ate too many peanuts and got a tummy ache. Would you prefer a small, smaller or smallest tummy ache?" The discussion was followed by a snack—a peanut, a raisin, a slice of apple, and a happy face cookie.

FOLLOW-UP ACTIVITIES: During free activity time some of the children drew pictures about their shared experience in the language center. They chose words to describe their pictures as noted under each illustration.

To further develop this theme the teacher labeled three sections of one table, big, bigger, biggest and three sections of another table, small, smaller, smallest. She grouped common items into three member sets of varying sizes (e.g., wooden spoons, candles, shoe laces, cereal boxes, plastic glasses). Children were asked to select one set and place its members in proper order on one of the two tables. When they had finished ordering by size comparisons, the children were asked to repeat each category aloud (i.e., big, bigger, biggest, or small, smaller, smallest).

Some children wanted to play a game in which the teacher blindfolded one child at a time, placed an object in each hand, and asked the child to identify the objects by name and size.

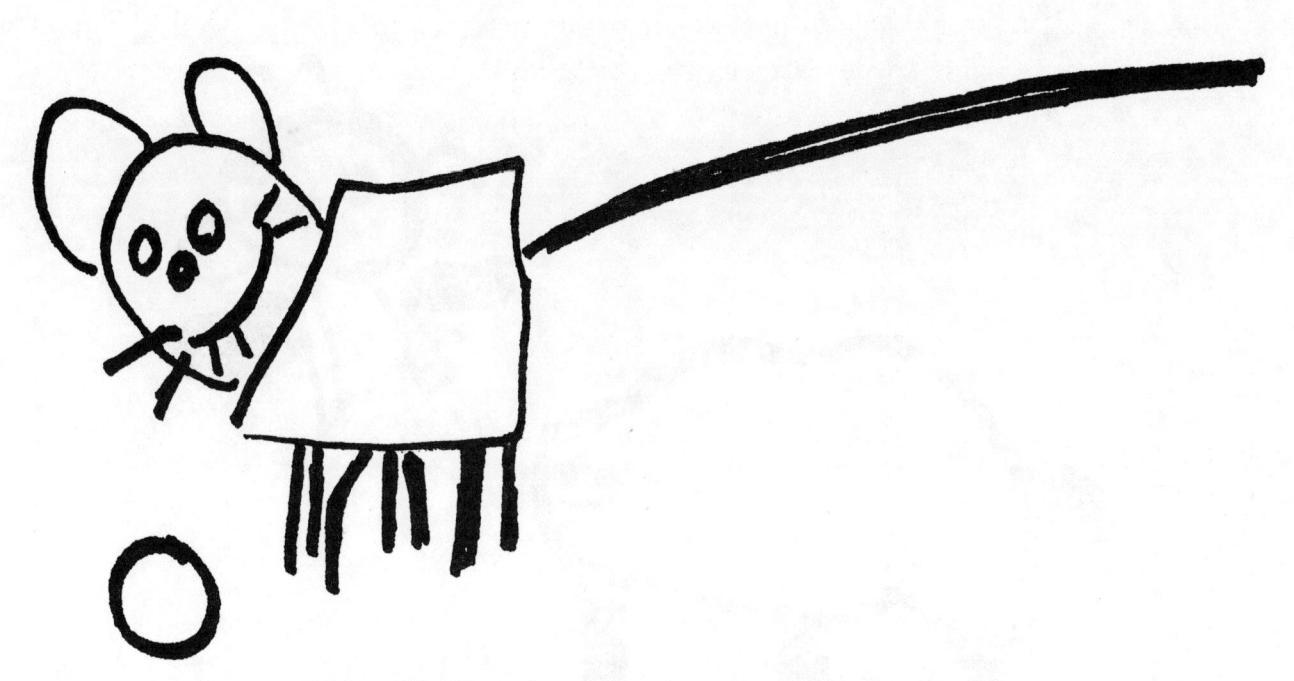

"The big lion is going to eat the little egg."

"This little bee is leaving his hive to live in an apartment in the city."

"This big cheetah is going to attack the little bee. I think the bee will sting him!"

"This is a big circle and this is a small circle—or maybe they are eggs cracking open."

Theme 3

TITLE: **"Families"**

PURPOSE: The teacher wanted children to understand the concept of family in its immediate and broader context (i.e., family nucleus through a family of nations) to promote social interaction, sensitivity toward other people, oral communication and language development.

MATERIALS: Paper, magic markers, and the book, *Grandfather and I* by Helen E. Buckley.

PROCEDURE: In preparation for sharing time, the teacher and children sent the following note home:

> Dear Mom and Dad,
>
> We are studying families this week and I would appreciate your spending a little time with me tonight talking about yourselves. I would like to know what you wanted to be as a child, when you grew up; what you like to do; and what makes you angry and happy? If you could make one wish come true, what would it be?
>
> I would like to bring in some items for sharing tomorrow, things that tell or show something about our family. Also, I would like to bring into class a small family photograph for our family tree. I promise to take good care of everything. Thank you for your help.
>
> Love,
>
> _____(child's name)

During sharing time, children eagerly took turns showing and telling about family items. The teacher encouraged questions and good listening during these exchanges. Family photographs were hung on a large bulletin board in a family tree arrangement to emphasize the concept of a classroom family. Children placed their pictures on the trunk, limbs or branches. At the conclusion of sharing time, the teacher suggested that sometimes changes occur in a family structure that affect family members: happy things like the birth of a child, sad things like illness, and things that can be both sad and happy like big sisters and brothers going off to college or moving away into a new experience. She stressed the importance of sharing and caring about one another . . . "and that is a good feeling, isn't it?" During story time, the teacher read the book, *Grandfather and I*.

FOLLOW-UP ACTIVITIES: During free activity time some of the children drew pictures about their shared experience in the language center. They chose words to describe their pictures as noted under each illustration.

To further develop this theme, the teacher read the fairy tale, *The Little Red Hen* to the class and invited the children to act out the story using their own words to describe the events. The children talked about the industrious little hen, her unhelpful friends, and the lesson they had learned. Words like cooperation, friendship, and sharing were brought into the conversation. Some children felt the little red hen should give her friends a second chance by sharing the bread—others felt she should have eaten every crumb.

The teacher also provided an opportunity for children to cut and paste pictures of families going places and doing things. The teacher pointed out similarities and differences in family customs, dress, nationalities, and racial origins.

"This is Daddy smoking a pipe. It doesn't smell good to me."

"My mommy is pretty but she doesn't like to clean the house."

"Mommy and Daddy would like to have a little guinea pig."

"This is my family. We all love shoes. I am the little one at the bottom."

108 FEATHERS IN MY CAP

Theme 4

TITLE: **"The President"**

PURPOSE: This experience was designed to take advantage of an election year to introduce children to basic aspects of the American system of government: the two party system, the electoral process, the importance of the presidency, the first family, and the White House.

The teacher believed that young children could understand the fundamentals of a campaign if the information was presented from a child's perspective. By conducting a mock election, she hoped that children would learn something about issues, campaigning, and personalities, as well as respect for the commitment and dedication that goes with the office.

MATERIALS: Campaign material cut from newspapers and magazines, a large cardboard appliance box, paints, and ingredients for a post-election victory cake.

PROCEDURE: The classroom was decorated with campaign material cut from newspapers and magazines or obtained from campaign headquarters. The teacher cut out a donkey and an elephant and explained their significance. A large cardboard carton was transformed into an election booth with the help of pictures, drawings and an American flag. After reviewing issues, backgrounds, and personality attributes of each candidate and his family, children stepped inside the booth and voted for the candidate of their choice. After voting, the children decided their winner by a show of hands and planned a victory celebration. The teacher and her friends baked a cake in the shape of a donkey.

FOLLOW-UP ACTIVITIES: During free activity time some of the children drew pictures about their shared experience in the language center. They chose words to describe their pictures as noted under each illustration.

To further develop this theme the teacher suggested that the children write a letter to the first family to request pictures of the White House and some of its residents. A dictated letter containing personal pictures signed by each student was mailed to The White House. A short time later the children received an envelope from Washington, D.C. containing a personal letter, a picture of the first family, a picture of the White House and a little "something" for each child.

"This is the President. He is happy because he is going on a vacation."

110   FEATHERS IN MY CAP

"This is the President. He knows how to plant peanuts."

Amy

"This is Amy Carter clapping her hands."

LEA In Classroom And Home

"This is a picture of President Carter."

"Mrs. Carter is very pretty. She has pierced ears. She loves earrings."

Theme 5

TITLE: **"Thanksgiving"**

PURPOSE: As part of an ongoing unit entitled "Preparing for Thanksgiving," this theme was directed toward life in a new land, emphasizing the contributions Pilgrims and Indians made to early America. The three-part unit included: A Voyage on the Mayflower, Pilgrims and Indians, and The First Thanksgiving. The teacher hoped that children would develop their appreciation of historical concepts, their heritage, brotherhood, and learn new words (e.g., *harvest, feast, mayflower, canoe, wampum, pheasant, deer, log cabin, freedom*).

MATERIALS: Clay, macaroni, construction paper, string, paints, and pillow cases to be used as Indian costumes (slit at the neck and fringed at the bottom).

PROCEDURE: The teacher talked about early Indian and Pilgrim life during the week preceding her presentation, emphasizing the way the country looked to the first American settlers, their first meeting with the Indians, differences in speech, appearance, and customs and how Pilgrims and Indians found ways to communicate and cooperate. She also discussed how the Indians were displaced later when the settlers moved onto their land, and how this led to conflicts which still exist today.

During the week children made Indian costumes (by painting the pillow cases with Indian symbols and designs), pottery, wampum (from large macaroni shells), log cabins (from strips of construction paper), feathers, Pilgrim hats, and corn bread.

During sharing time, the teacher and children acted out the story of the first Thanksgiving. As the teacher narrated the dramatization, the children went through the motions of planting and harvesting crops, hunting and fishing, and preparing for the feast. Everyone wanted to sit at the head of the table!

FOLLOW-UP ACTIVITIES: During free activity time some of the children drew pictures about their shared experience in the language center. They chose words to describe their pictures as noted under each illustration.

To further develop this theme the teacher suggested that the children prepare their own Thanksgiving dinner. They decided to make vegetable soup, baked apples, corn bread, and pumpkin pie. Each child was asked to contribute a food item and to think about one thing that he/she was especially thankful for. As thank you's were shared, the teacher lit a Thanksgiving candle for this special day.

"This turkey is running into a barn. The farmer can't catch him."

114   FEATHERS IN MY CAP

"This Indian chief is angry. He has lost his bow and arrow."

"The boy is in his teepee. His horse is waiting for him. The horse likes to wear feathers, too."

"The Pilgrims are on the Mayflower. They want to go to Florida. They are good friends."

Theme 6

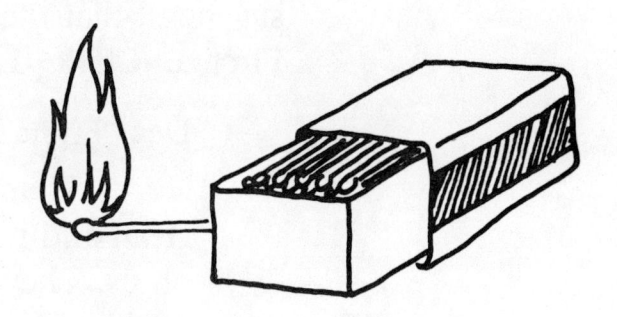

TITLE:	**"A Trip To The Firehouse"**
PURPOSE:	As part of an ongoing unit entitled "Community Friends," the teacher planned a trip to a local firehouse to provide a firsthand "community friends in action" experience. She hoped that children would begin to appreciate the importance of contributing to community life, acquire new understandings and ideas, expand their knowledge about how a community functions, and practice good listening habits and good manners.
MATERIALS:	Visual aids relating to community helpers and their activities; wood, books, paints, and cotton swabs.
PROCEDURE:	The teacher read *Hercules* by Hardie Gramatky before the children left for the firehouse. A brief discussion included new words, what the children were to see on their trip, the importance of good manners, the consequences of playing with matches, what causes fire, and what makes fire burn. During their trip to the firehouse the children were escorted through sleeping, recreational, and working quarters. They were taken into the dispatch room to listen to firemen talk, and they were allowed to sit in the pumper and hook and ladder trucks. The visit was highlighted by an animated film on fire fighting. Each child was given a fire hat before leaving.
FOLLOW-UP ACTIVITIES:	During free activity time some of the children drew pictures about their shared experience in the language center. They chose words to describe their pictures as noted under each illustration.

LEA In Classroom And Home

To further develop this theme the teacher suggested that the children dictate a thank you note to Fireman Clark. The children wrote:

Dear Fireman Clark,

Thank you for your firehouse. It is very clean and noisy. Thank you for trying your hats on us. They are very heavy. When we grow up we could be firemen and drive the hook and ladder truck with you. You sure had a lot of stuff in the ambulance. One thing, where is the dog that lives in the firehouse?

Love,
The Fours

"I loved that great big fire truck!"

ACTIVITIES FOR CHAPTER 3:

Language Experience in the Home

Implementing language activities in the home can provide worlds of pleasure between parent and child as well as important learning experiences. The following themes and picture story illustrations represent a few of the many ways that children can profit from language experience in the home:

"I just made six trouble dolls in this picture. One doll is under my pillow."

Theme 7

TITLE: **"My Trouble Dolls"**

PURPOSE: A parent wanted to reinforce language experience, spend meaningful time with her child, and stimulate language development.

MATERIALS: Clothespins, yarn, old scraps of material, a small cardboard container with a lid, strips of colored paper, and paint if desired.

PROCEDURE: The parent told the following story to her child:

> "There is a story that is passed down to Indian children that when a child has a problem, before going to sleep she removes one trouble doll from her trouble basket, whispers her problem to the doll and places her under her pillow. While the child sleeps the doll tries to solve the problem."

Since a trouble doll can only solve one problem at a time, the parent suggested that the child make seven dolls, one for each night of the week. Together the parent and child made seven little dolls from clothespins, scraps of material and yarn. They made a trouble basket by covering a container with strips of colored paper woven into a basket design, and the trouble basket began to take shape. As the parent and child were working together, they discussed each of their troubles. In the process of sharing these special moments together, the parent and child discovered a new way to communicate feelings of love and understanding.

"On Saturday me and my mom bake cookies. My dad eats them all up."

Theme 8

TITLE: **"Gingerbread Friends"**

PURPOSE: A parent wanted to reinforce language experience; provide an experience that would be fun for both parent and child; introduce new words to the child; and practice measurement skills.

MATERIALS: Ingredients for gingerbread cookies and the story *The Gingerbread Man*.

PROCEDURE: The parent and the child decided to make gingerbread people using the following recipe:

> 2 tablespoons water
> ½ cup brown sugar
> 1 teaspoon cinnamon
> ½ teaspoon nutmeg
> ½ teaspoon ginger
> ½ teaspoon salt
> ½ teaspoon baking soda
> 3 cups whole wheat flour
> ½ cup powdered milk

Mix water and dry ingredients together. Add flour and milk and stir into a good dough (add a bit more flour if too sticky). Shape dough into people and decorate with raisins. Bake 10 minutes at 375°.

LEA In Classroom And Home

While the cookies were baking, the parent read *The Gingerbread Man* aloud. While Mom was cleaning up, she suggested that her child make some gingerbread picture stories to add to his language experience notebook. The outcome was delightful (and the cookies delicious)!

"No one can catch this gingerbread man. He's too fast!"

124 FEATHERS IN MY CAP

Theme 9

TITLE: **"It's Snowing In My House"**

PURPOSE: A parent wanted to reinforce language experience. Understanding the importance of daily reading to one's child, this parent decided to make the story, *A Snowy Day* by Ezra Keats, a special project for her child.

MATERIALS: The book *A Snowy Day,* colored construction paper, a box of Ivory Flakes, an egg beater, and white shelf paper cut to fit language experience notebook.

PROCEDURE: As the parent read this delightful story about a little boy experiencing the pleasures of snow, her child began to imagine that she too was a part of that wonderful world: snowballs in pockets, colorful scarf and pointed cap, tracks in the snow and drifts to play in! Eager to expand upon her child's enthusiasm, the parent suggested that the child make her own snow by beating Ivory Flakes with a small amount of water. When the snow was ready for finger painting on white shelf paper, the child made her own snowy day pictures. By adding shapes and objects cut from colored paper, the child gave color and life to her landscapes.

"The snowman wants to ride on that sled but he's afraid he'll roll off. I didn't make a sun so he won't melt."

"The little girl is going to make snowballs with her cat, Tina."

FEATHERS IN MY CAP

Theme 10

TITLE:	**"Dromedaries Weren't Always Happy"**
PURPOSE:	A parent wanted to reinforce language experience. She selected the book *The Happy Dromedary* by Berniece Freschet to provide an imaginative and innovative setting for language experience picture stories. The parent also hoped to acquaint her child with a desert environment and one of the desert's very good friends, the camel.
MATERIALS:	The book *The Happy Dromedary*, one meat tray (may be obtained at the supermarket), sand or corn meal, colored construction paper, toothpicks, and clay.
PROCEDURE:	Parent and child learned about the evolution of a dromedary from clunky feet that sank in the sand to the proud and dignified animal he is today.

The story tells us that things were not easy for the dromedary in the beginning. Unlike other animals, he wanted to live in the desert and he was willing to endure mockery and isolation from the other animals until his wish was granted. With the help of the animal king, he accepted his uniqueness and was gradualy tailored to life on the desert.

The book opened exciting channels of communication between parent and child: they discussed what it is like to be different, the meaning of courage, patience and hope, the necessity of change.

LEA In Classroom And Home

The parent and child decided to make a diorama together. After filling a meat tray with sand and cactus plants (drawn from colored construction paper and fastened to the tray with toothpicks), the child made his camel from clay. Like the dromedary in the story, his camel had a hump and flat feet that were large enough for long walks across the desert! On the following morning, the child found a little cactus plant on his bedside table.

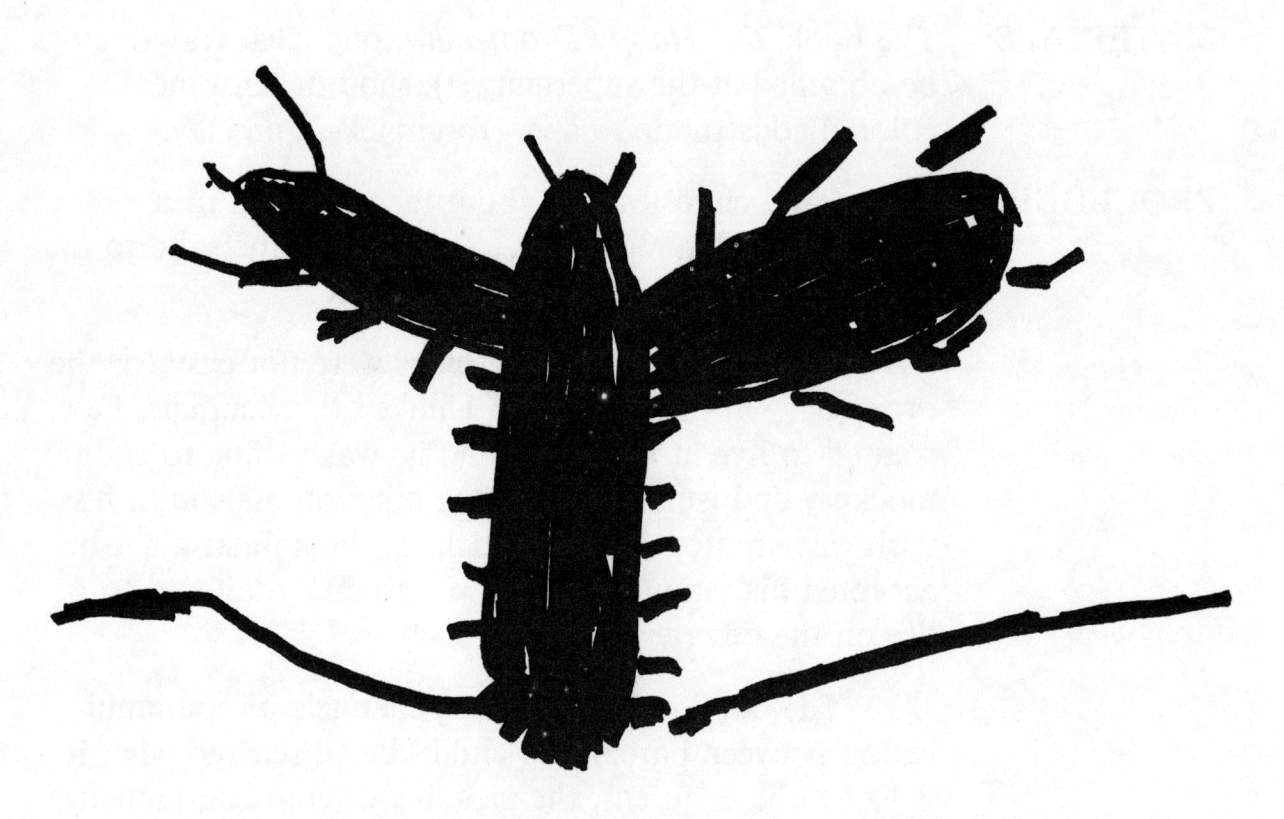

"This giant cactus has prickles that hurt. There may be some water inside. The cactus belongs to a camel."

"I think the dromedary can't find any friends in the desert. Maybe he should live in the woods."

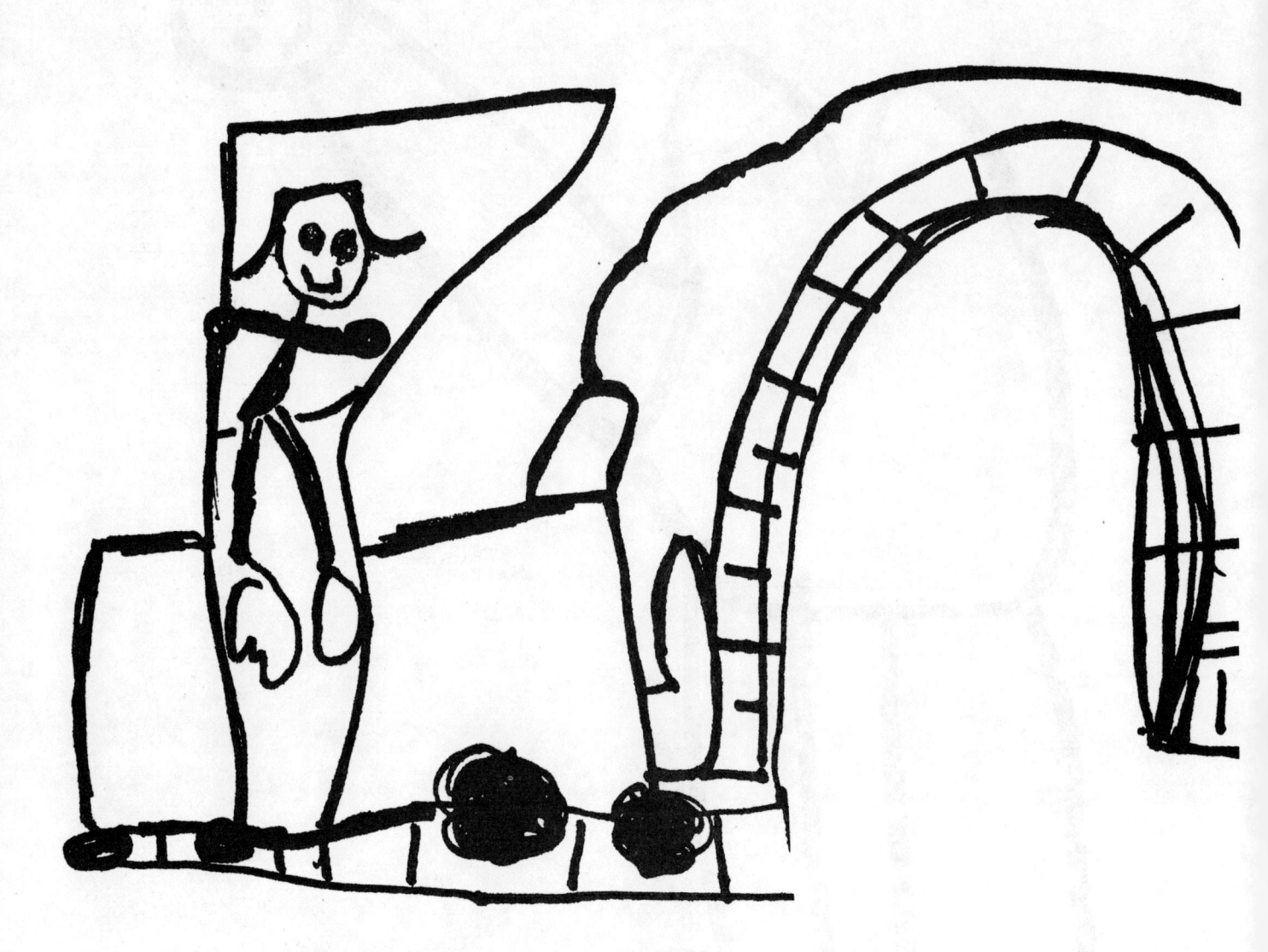

"When I grow up I want to be a train girl with lots of tracks."

Theme 11

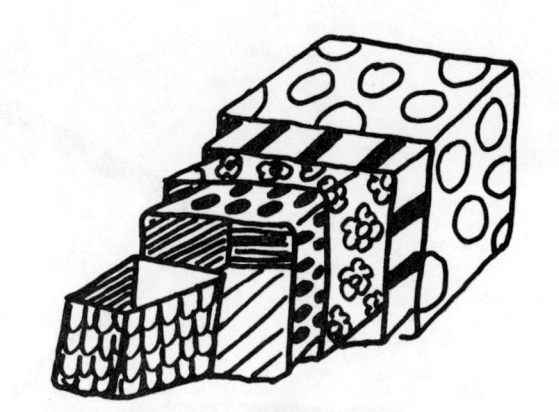

TITLE: **"Boxes of Fun"**

PURPOSE: A parent wanted to reinforce language experience. Since his child was fascinated with trains, one parent decided that this would be an appropriate theme and a great deal of fun for his child.

MATERIALS: Boxes of different sizes, paint, twine, construction paper, and the book *The Little Engine That Could* by Watty Piper.

PROCEDURE: After reading the delightful classic, *The Little Engine That Could,* the parent suggested that his child make her own train out of cardboard boxes. As the child arranged the boxes in horizontal order, she decided that one car would be the engine, one a caboose, one for passengers, one for dolls, one for coal, and one for candy.

The child painted each box a different color while her father connected them with strong twine. Large decorative black wheels were pasted on each box to add a sense of movement to the train. Finally, when the train was dry and ready for passengers and good things to eat, the little girl labeled each car and filled the train for its long trip over the mountain.

"I can't think which box to hide in!"

Theme 12

TITLE: **"Cindy the Caterpillar"**

PURPOSE: A parent wanted to reinforce language experience; stimulate interest in nature; provide a long term project that would occupy a young child while providing important scientific concepts (e.g., the evolution from caterpillar to moth and comparisons and characteristics of each form).

MATERIALS: Small pieces of flannel, a flannel board (cover a bulletin board or plywood with a piece of flannel or burlap), a mayonnaise jar, leaves and a branch, and colored markers to add personality to flannel board figures.

PROCEDURE: Knowing how much her child loved caterpillars, this parent told the following story about the metamorphosis of one little caterpillar, using flannel board figures to illustrate a caterpillar, a little girl, a cocoon, and a moth:

> "Some time ago there was a caterpiillar named Cindy. Unlike other caterpillars, her best friend was a little girl named Sara. Instead of eating lots and lots of leaves in preparation for her long sleep, Cindy sat on her favorite leaf and watched Sara playing with her toys. One day Sara told Cindy that if she would get busy and eat all the leaves she could possibly hold, Sara would take care of her all winter while she slept. Not long after, when Cindy had shed her skin for the

LEA In Classroom And Home

eighth time, she knew it was time to sleep. Sara tucked her safely in a jar next to her favorite leaf, and Cindy spun a magnificent cocoon around herself on a cozy branch. She closed her eyes thinking about how pleased Sara would be to see her new clothes in the spring — her beautiful wings just made for flying. But inside she would always be the same Cindy. Months later, Sara watched her little friend slowly spread and flutter her new wings as if to say, 'It's time for me to go, Sara,' and Sara knew that she would come back again.''

Together, parent and child prepared a home for a caterpillar. A mayonnaise jar (with holes punctured in the lid), some moistened leaves, and a stick provided a perfect setting for observing the process to its completion. "Cindy the Caterpillar" was the little girl's longest language experience story.

"The little girl is wishing she could have the caterpillar. The caterpillar wants to go in the house after she eats the leaf."

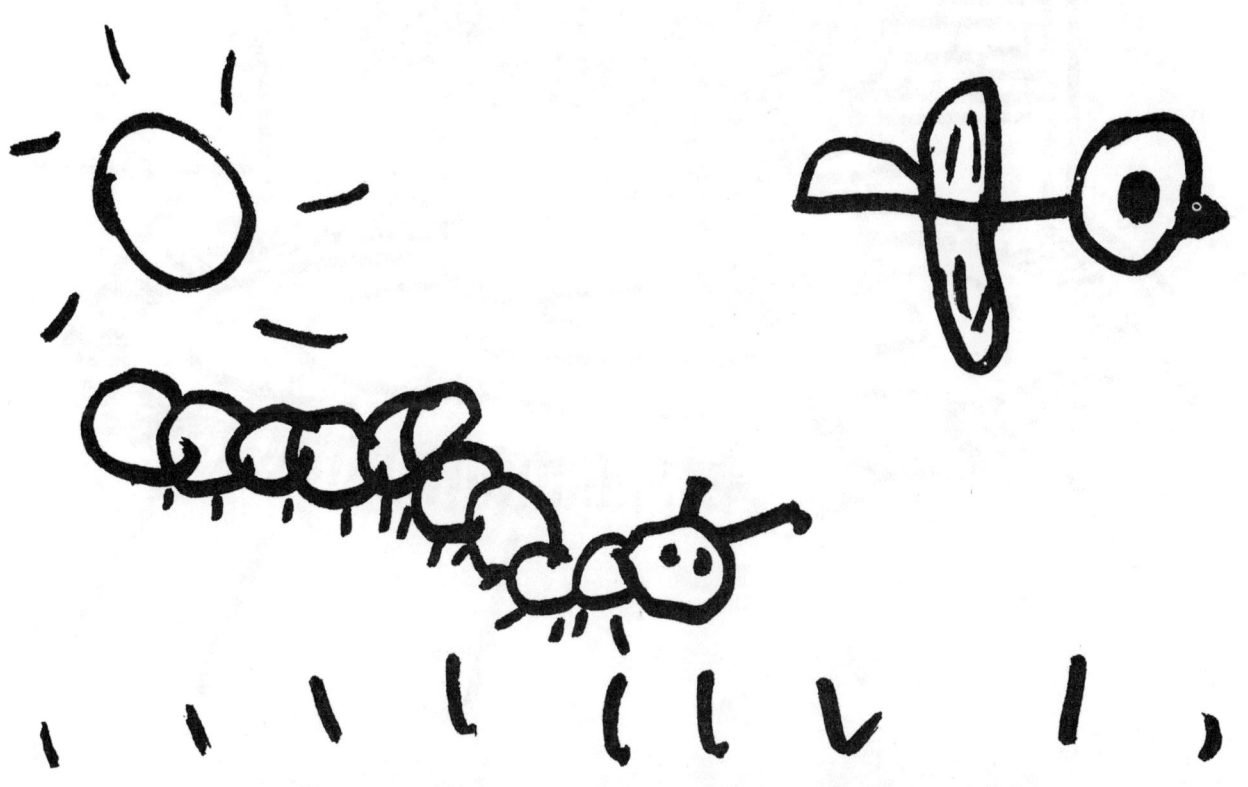

"The caterpillar is walking and the bird is flying. When the caterpillar can fly it will be friends with the bird.

LEA In Classroom And Home

FEATHERS IN MY CAP

Chapter 4

CLASSROOM ACTIVITIES IN THE LANGUAGE ARTS

The following section offers supplemental activities in reading, listening, speaking, writing and art that may be used with language experience projects or integrated into a general language arts curriculum. In addition, 20 worksheets provide an introduction to picture stories and key word activities for use at the early childhood level.

INTEGRATING LANGUAGE ARTS ACTIVITIES IN THE CLASSROOM:

READING

If one looks at early childhood learning experiences as links in a developmental chain, reading is seen as one part of the communication process, interwoven with and influenced by many other forms of self-expression. The more children experience themselves through all facets of communication, the closer they will be to reading readiness.

Young children not only love to play games but they absorb a great deal while interacting with their peers. Once they have grasped directions, they will play a game over and over, waiting patiently or impatiently to win! When children play games, they are learning the discipline of following directions, step sequencing, conceptual understandings, new ideas, new words, patience, social skills, and what it feels like to be a winner, and how to take losing in stride.

The following activities are designed primarily for language experience, and it is hoped that teachers and parents will see the value of developing reading readiness activity games from their own imagination and creativity.

Activity 1: Key Word Charts

These charts are used for sight word recognition in connection with *Step 4* of language experience when the teacher reads an original story with her class.

Key words may be defined as descriptive words taken from original stories for the purpose of developing sight word recognition and recall. They are words that can be illustrated in order to provide contextual clues to word meanings. The teacher and the children can select them. The following categories may be useful in selecting key words:

Category	Examples
words that denote living things:	tree, whale, fox, bug
action words:	run, swim, jump, hop, walk
family words:	mother, father, sister, brother, uncle
size words:	big, little, small, large, fat, long
shape words:	square, triangle, circle, rectangle
words that describe inanimate objects:	chair, book, rug
state of being words:	sad, happy, tired, hungry, scared
proper names:	Mary, Tom, Ohio

Instructions for making key word charts:

1. When a title has been agreed upon for a language experience book, the teacher asks the children to assist in making a key word chart for special word friends. The teacher has a posterboard clipped to an easel or to a multi-purpose stand. If the teacher anticipates the need for more than four words on a chart, she should use the standard 22" x 28" size; for fewer words, 11" x 13" will suffice. Poster-

board can be purchased in assorted colors at most drug stores with school supply sections. In addition to its durability, posterboard has the advantage of easy storage—it can be slipped behind a book shelf when not in use. If posterboard becomes a luxury because of budgetary considerations, newsprint may be substituted which can be purchased in 18" x 21" reams. Since paper is difficult to store over a long period of time, the teacher may want to run masking tape along the top of each sheet and fasten the completed charts to a wall fixture. An alternative solution is to string up a clothesline and use clothespins as fasteners.

2. The teacher prints the title of the book in the top center of the key word chart, and a number in the upper right hand corner. The number corresponds to the number on a group story assigned by the teacher upon the completion of each book. I recommend colored markers for printing because they are bright and visible. Words should be clearly and neatly printed in standard upper-lower case letters. (If the teacher finds she cannot print without running her lines up or downhill she can try drawing horizontal lines in pencil before she begins).

3. As words are selected, the teacher prints key words in vertical order, leaving ample space between each word. As she prints each word she identifies the letters by name (e.g., s-u-n). She repeats the word again with the children before proceeding to the next word.

4. Illustrations for each key word are drawn by the children in vertical order on the right hand margin.

5. During an instructional period on the following day, the teacher should review the key words using the following format:

   a. As the teacher points to each word, the children read each word and picture friend in sequential order from top to bottom.

   b. The teacher isolates the entire word group by covering the pictures with a piece of plain white paper. The children then read the words without picture clues.

   c. The teacher randomly selects a key word to isolate from the remaining words and pictures by using a window cutout covering made of white posterboard.

   d. On subsequent days, the teacher reinforces language experience words through word chart review and activity games at the language center.

Illustrations for Key Word Charts:

LEA In Classroom And Home

Activity 2: Group Word Banks

As key words become familiar to young children, they want to work with words during individualized experiences in the language center. A group word bank allows children to deposit and withdraw key words for informal work-play experiences. These banks serve to facilitate the retention of key words related to original group stories. The children learn responsibility for the orderly maintenance of classroom equipment as well as the rudimentary beginnings in filing and coding material. Working with words may also lead to printing experiences using familiar key words or word sentences for supplemental activities in the language center.

Instructions for making group word banks:

1. The teacher obtains a 4" x 6" or 5" x 8" file box and several packages of index cards in white or pastel colors. (Stories can be color-coded).

2. Each language experience story is given a section in the container. Since it is important that children learn to use the word banks with minimal assistance, the teacher should make sectional dividers that can be understood by children. If there is not enough room for an entire title, the teacher condenses the title to one word if possible. She prints the word and the group story code number on a sectional divider in the file box.

3. The teacher prepares one set consisting of index cards for each key word on a chart. She prints the key words on two cards and makes a picture of the key word on a third card. In this

way children can play matching card games with two or more sets of cards, matching word-to-word cards and word-to-picture cards. On the upper right hand corner of each card, the teacher prints the group story card number so that children can return them to the proper place in the word bank.

Illustrations for key word banks:

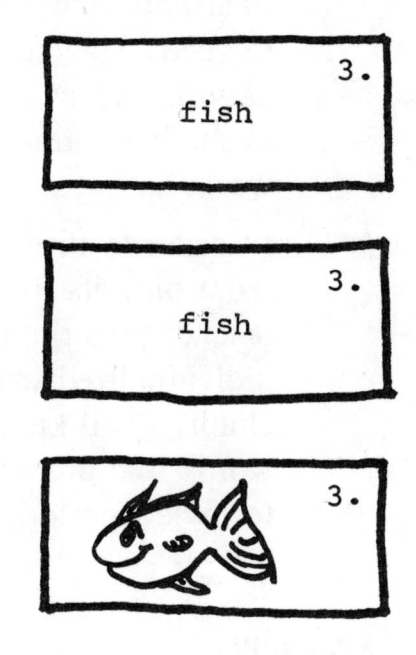

Activity 3: Individual Word Banks

An excellent way to reinforce sight reading skills is to make an individual word bank for each child to take home, practice, and return to class on a designated day. The teacher can include familiar words such as instant words and sight words (e.g., colors, days of the week, names of the months, holidays) in these word banks.

Instructions for making individual word banks:

1. The teacher obtains several packages of 5" x 8" index cards (use unlined side for printing words) and a small envelope for each child (suggested size: 6" x 9").

2. She prints the name of each child and the words "My Word Bank" on each envelope.

3. Explaining how to use these banks, she tells the children that they will get a small sticker on their envelope for every five word cards learned. The teacher emphasizes the words *deposit* and *withdrawal* as she deposits new cards in the bank and withdraws them for practice work.

4. In order to distinguish new sets of sight words from old sets (those previously learned), the teacher underlines previously learned words in individualized word banks. In this way, children will know which words to learn—those words that are not underlined. It is important to review periodically all words in the banks.

Illustrations:

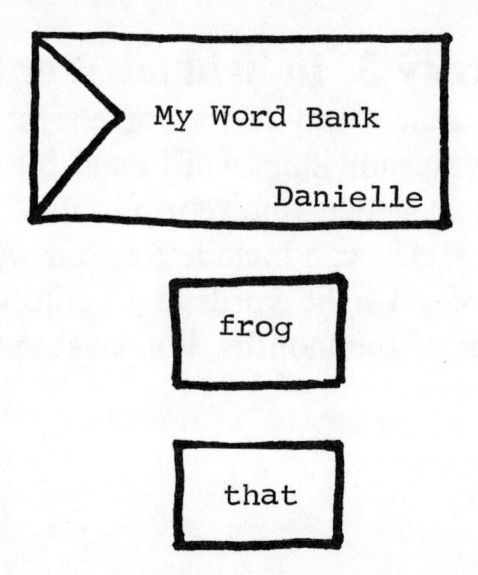

My Word Bank
Danielle

frog

that

Activity 4: A game: What Am I?

The teacher tells the children that she is going to describe a word on their word chart(s) giving some clues to its identity. She might say, for example, "I am thinking of a word on the chart that is an animal, soft, and gray," etc. She continues until a child has guessed the word. That child then selects a word and gives clues. The teacher may want to use several word charts to challenge the children and review previously learned words.

Activity 5: A game: Tell A Tall Tale

The teacher tells the children that they are about to tell a tall tale about a key word. She points to one word on the key chart such as *elephant,* and begins a story. "Once there was an elephant walking slowly through the woods. He was going to the _____." (child completes the thought by pointing to a key word). The teacher continues to develop the story stopping from time to time for a key word supplied by children. As a story develops, children delight in the absurdity of using key words out of context. To extend the game, the teacher should use more than one key word chart. It is also useful to jot down tall tale story ideas before beginning the game. For example, the above story might be completed in the following way: Once there was an elephant walking through the woods. He was going to the *zoo,* where he met a *giraffe.* The giraffe said, "Elephant why are you *pink*?" The elephant said, "I'm not pink, I'm *green*!" The giraffe said, "Then you're not an *elephant*!" (The key words are italicized.)

Activity 6: A game: A Tisket, A Tasket, A Key Word In Your Basket

The group sits in a circle; the teacher puts a key word taken from the word bank into a small basket and selects a child to deliver the "message" to a friend in the circle. The child drops the message in a friend's lap, the friend stands up, reads the word card and returns it to the teacher. While each child is taking a turn, the group may hum or sing a familiar tune such as "A Tisket, A Tasket." The teacher may want to combine large motor activities with this game by asking a child to hop, skip, gallop, tiptoe, or waddle around the circle.

Activity 7: A game: Going Fishing

The teacher cuts out fish drawn on colored construction paper. She prints a key word on each fish, attaches a paper clip to each tail and puts them in a clothes basket. She asks the children to make a fishing pole from a tree branch; she then attaches string to each pole and ties a magnet to the end of the string. Seated in a circle around a pretend fish pond, each child gets a chance to catch a "fish" word, read it, and throw it back into the pond.

FEATHERS IN MY CAP

Activity 8: A game: Call-A-Friend

Children are seated in a circle. Each one has a pretend phone. The teacher selects a key word and whispers it to the first child who whispers it to a friend seated next to him. The last child in the circle stands up, points to the word message on the key word chart and says the word out loud. That child moves into the first position. The game continues until everyone has had a turn. Children may want to make their own telephones for this game. On a piece of cardboard cut in the shape of a phone, children can print their own numbers and their names in the center ring.

Activity 9: A matching card game: The Terrible Troll

For this game, the teacher makes two sets of matching word cards taken from key word charts or magic feather caps. Using index cards, she prints at least twelve words and makes a duplicate set of the same words (total, twenty-four cards). On another index card, the teacher makes a picture of a terrible troll and labels this card "the terrible troll." Passing out all the cards to two players, the teacher instructs the children to alternate picking one card from each other's hand. Matching cards should be laid down, face up, on a table or on the floor as the game progresses. When all the other cards have been matched, one child will be left with the terrible troll card. Children should be encouraged to read the word cards to their teacher before leaving the game.

Activity 10: A game: Toss and Read

The teacher outlines five squares on a floor with masking tape. These squares should be large enough to catch a bean bag thrown from a distance of four or five feet. Inside each square, the teacher places a key word card taken from the word bank. Each child gets a turn to toss a bean bag and read the word in the square. Whoever tosses and reads twice without missing a square and a word is the first winner. The teacher might like to ask parents to make a bean bag for each child. This game may also be played with magic feather cap words.

Activity 11: A game: To Market To Market

The teacher places key words and instant words on small note paper in a multi-compartment billfold. Each child gets a turn to buy something from "the general store." Skipping to market from a group circle, a child reaches into the billfold and pulls out a key word while his classmates are singing, "To market, to market to buy a _____" (child reads the word). The game becomes more and more animated as the children proceed to select items that never could be purchased in a market.

FEATHERS IN MY CAP

Activity 12: An ongoing project: The Reading Tree

For this project, the teacher secures a large branch and places it in a dirt-filled flower pot, referring to it as "The Reading Tree." The tree is decorated with sight words that designate holidays, seasonal changes, language experience themes, key words, and instant words.

For example, in fall, the teacher may hang large colored leaves on the branch with key words and seasonal words such as "fall," "leaves," or "September." In winter, the teacher may hang snowflakes on the tree with key words, instant words or winter words such as "snowman," "cold," or "sled." On Valentine's day, she may change the decorations to hearts with special friendship words such as "love," "friend," "share," or "gift." In spring she may decorate the reading tree with blossoms and birds.

She can also make up games to reinforce sight word development. For example, she may have the children recite:

> Birdie in the tree,
> Birdie in the tree,
> Birdie find a key word,
> And bring it back to me.

Each child can take a turn being "birdie," select a key word, remove it from the tree, and read it aloud to the class.

LEA In Classroom And Home

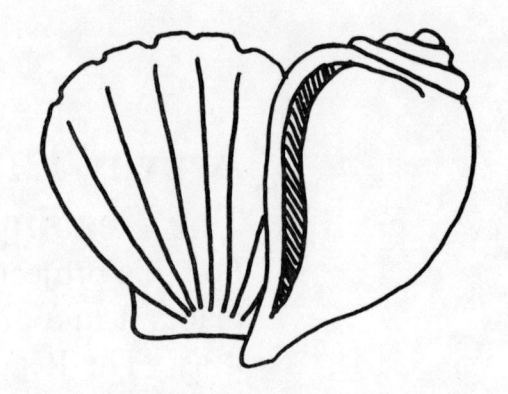

LISTENING

Listening, as a primary facet of the language arts, cannot be neglected in the early childhood years. As a young child listens to the words and thoughts of others, he is learning sound discrimination, critical listening skills, and new ways of expressing ideas. As he begins to define his own speech patterns, he is implicitly sorting out and comparing manifold ways of communicating. He may add his own meaning to a new word or idea but he continues to try out his new-found power until he finds the context to suit his meaning. As he increases his listening skills, he is increasing his language power.

Unfortunately aural development is often overshadowed by other more direct forms of communication, particularly in a large and active classroom. A young child does not always understand that he can raise his hand and say, "I can't hear that," or "I can't understand that." If he is sitting quietly and appears to be a part of the group, the teacher assumes that he is listening and comprehending.

Informal and formal tests can provide valuable indicators of listening facility, but these opportunities are not always available at the early childhood level, particularly in private schools. Inadequate attention to this crucial aspect of communication can leave indelible scars on a child's emotional and academic development.

There are many ways that a teacher can focus attention on listening skills and increase her own sensitivity to potential problems. A walk through the woods, a trip to a hatchery, a trip to a nature center, or playing listening games can heighten sound discrimination as well as increase aesthetic appreciation. As the child distinguishes between gentle and harsh sounds, and pleasant and unpleasant sounds, he is increasing his level of awareness and ability to communicate. As he learns to follow directions and to listen for retention and comprehension, he is acquiring fundamental skills that are essential to growth and development.

Activity 13: A Trip To An Animal Farm

A trip to an animal farm or a zoo can provide an excellent listening experience for young children. In discussing the trip, the teacher may ask "How do you think animals communicate with one another? What was your favorite animal sound? What kind of sound did the pig make when she got excited? What do you think the turkey and the duck were saying to each other?"

The teacher may play a listening record describing the sounds of a farm or a zoo (see Appendix). Children may want to duplicate the sound of a loud elephant, a grouchy monkey, a roaring lion, a screeching bird, or a gentle lamb.

Activity 14: A Trip To A City
A teacher may promote sound discrimination by taking the children on an imaginary trip to a city. She asks her children to help her make the sound of traffic whizzing over a bridge and zooming through a tunnel, the sounds of kitty cats after dark, subway trains and garbage trucks, street cleaners, and paper boys.

In their imaginary trip the teacher asks her children which sounds they liked the best, which the least, and why? Also, she may suggest the children think of ways that city people can turn down sound for a little while.

Activity 15: Country Sounds
As a similar activity, the class can take an imaginary trip to the country. Pointing out the quiet sounds of the country, such as rustling leaves, grazing cattle, bubbling brooks, and the occasional intrusion of a far off tractor or plane, the teacher can create a country mood. She might embellish the mood by saying, "I see Peter climbing a tree; there is Sandra picking flowers; and, oh, there are Jamie and Sally Ann climbing an oak tree; and, oh yes, way over there—it's Matt crossing the creek—whoops, splash!" At the conclusion of these experiences, she may ask her group whether they would prefer the noise of the city or the quietness of the countryside, and why? Hopefully, some of the children will see benefits to both places.

Activity 16: A game: Who Is Knocking At My Door?

The teacher improvises a door by using a mobile book shelf tall enough for a young child to hide behind without being seen by classmates. The child in hiding must guess who is knocking, saying, "Who is knocking at my door?" A classmate selected by the teacher responds, "I am." The child has two turns to guess who said, "I am."

Activity 17: A game: Fly, Pigeon, Fly

The teacher whispers a short message to a "pigeon friend" in the classroom, asking him to "fly, pigeon, fly." The child listens to the message, "flies" over to a corner of the classroom and returns with the same message. The child then repeats the message aloud to the class. The teacher may want to expand upon this game by requesting that "pigeons" touch several items before their return, such as, "Touch something soft, something hard, and something yellow." This is an excellent game to use for teaching attention to directions and for sharpening critical listening skills. It is important that children cooperate by listening quietly while each child gets a turn.

Activity 18: Baby Steps and Giant Steps

Children must learn to listen for instructions and follow directions in this game, also. The teacher (the giant) stands on one end of the room and the children (little Jacks) on the other. The teacher tells each child that he may take _____ (gives number) baby or giant steps toward her. The child must always respond with "Giant, may I," before taking the steps. As children advance toward the teacher, one child will get close enough to touch the teacher-giant who leads a merry chase back to the starting point.

Activity 19: Listen to Mr. Gumpy

The teacher can use the delightful book *Mr. Gumpy's Outing,* by John Burningham, to train young children in listening for comprehension and sequential ordering. (The book won England's Kate Greenaway Medal in 1970).

> The problem with Mr. Gumpy is that he just couldn't say no. One day he went out on his boat for a quiet row when one by one his little animal and people friends asked to be included in the outing. Although he cautioned each friend to behave in the boat, a chain reaction was set off when the goat kicked and everyone fell into the river. But kind Mr. Gumpy invited his friends to tea, and every reader feels a part of that tea party.

The teacher can ask a lot of "why" or "what would happen if," questions to facilitate comprehension. She can also encourage sequential alertness by asking children if they can remember what happened next, and by reading with the children rather than to them by asking, "Who did Mr. Gumpy tell the cat not to chase?", etc.

Activity 20: Colors On Parade

The teacher might also like to use a quality activity record such as *Learning Basic Skills Through Music,* by Hap Palmer, to encourage good listening. In this particular record there is a song called *Colors* that requires children (who have assumed the role of colors) to stand up and sit down to instructions. The teacher can have her class act out this record by giving each child a piece of colored construction paper to correspond to the colors in the song. They will enjoy the activity as they learn to listen for instructions. Other songs on this record that require listening and body coordination skills include *"The Elephant," "Put Your Hands Up In The Air",* and *"Marching Around The Alphabet."* For a list of additional records that are useful in language experience activities, see Appendix.

SPEAKING

A young child's oral language facility is fundamental to the communication process. As children build confidence in their ability to communicate, they build confidence in their ability to function as independent human beings. If they perceive their environment as accepting and reinforcing, they will experience the freedom requisite to maturational development and original thinking. In a supportive environment, short phrases will grow into sentences, anxious verbalizations will become invested with relaxed humor and shy utterances will blossom into open, creative expression. The child will grow as his ability to communicate opens new corridors to self-realization and expansion. As oral language abilities develop and expand, children will be able to read with greater confidence and proficiency.

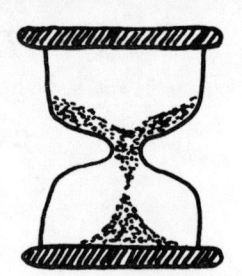

Activity 21: Show and Tell

This activity has long been a favorite with young children. It is important that teachers view Show and Tell as a valuable oral language opportunity because it promotes spontaneous dialogue, inquisitiveness, and social interaction. One interesting way to organize a Show and Tell experience is to have children bring something from home for a "relic museum" in the classroom. Children are told that the item must be unique, (not valuable) and brought in a surprise bag. During sharing time, children guess what the relic is by being given oral clues and feeling the item inside the bag. Each child should be given ample time to discuss the origins and purpose of an item before placing it in the museum.

Activity 22: A Pet Show

What better way to generate conversation than to have a pet show in school! After setting up preliminary guidelines, the teacher invites each child to bring a pet to class (a stuffed animal will be fine). The children may want to send a written invitation to another class. On the day of the pet show, each child walks his pet around a circle. Then, standing his pet on an orange crate platform, he tells its name, what kind of a pet it is, what it eats and something special about its habits. After each presentation, the pet and its owner receive a blue ribbon prize. (The teacher should have a pet "stand-in" for the child who forgets his pet).

Activity 23: Hansels and Gretels

The teacher may choose creative dramatics for language enrichment experiences. She may, for example, have her class act out the classic *Hansel and Gretel,* using their own dialogue to express the story. After listening to a recorded version of *Hansel and Gretel* (see Appendix), children select parts that have particular meaning to them, such as the main characters, the mother and father, the witch, a cat, the sandman, birds, strawberries, and gingerbread people. There is something for everyone in *Hansel and Gretel,* and with simple props and some encouragement, children will step into fairy-tale land.

An exciting follow-up to this activity might be making a real gingerbread cottage. The teacher and children make a gingerbread cake, slice it into two or three layers and decorate it with whipped cream, jelly beans and foil-wrapped candy kisses.

Activity 24: A Monkey's Tail

A teacher can also develop oral language skills through story-telling techniques such as this one.

Begin a story with a descriptive opening sentence like, "Once there was a monkey with a very long tail. His tail was so long, he could scarcely _____. He wished so badly that he could _____, but alas, he was just too _____. But one day the monkey went to visit a _____, who told him to _____. The monkey lived happily ever after." Ask the children to fill in the story using their own words.

Activity 25: Phone A Friend

Using two play phones, the teacher sets up a classroom dialogue between two friends. She tells the friends that she would like to record their voices while they are chatting together. Children will soon forget about the tape recorder and enter into spontaneous dialogue. They will be surprised and pleased when the teacher plays back their voices. To expand upon this activity, children may record favorite songs or finger plays for play-back pleasure.

Activity 26: Puppet Pigs

In a dramatic situation, it is not unusual for young children to feel more comfortable talking behind puppets than talking in front of peers. Fairy tales provide excellent content for puppet shows. Children will listen to a favorite tale over and over again with the enthusiasm of an opening night audience. One effective way to present a fairy tale such as *The Three Pigs* is to draw the puppet figures on posterboard, color them with magic marker, and then staple them to empty wrapping paper rolls or other long objects. The figures should be large and colorful enough to be seen by a young audience. The teacher can read the story, play a recording of the fairy tale or tape her own version before children put on their puppet show. "A Little Theatre" made from a sturdy cardboard box can provide the perfect setting for "Puppet Pigs." The box can be cut and decorated in imaginative ways and used over and over again for different kinds of puppet shows.

WRITING

There is no specific time for children to begin writing, but it is important to begin training during the early years. One way to strengthen eye-hand coordination is to provide manipulative activities that require fine muscle control such as working with tinker toys, stringing beads, dressing oneself, or cutting and pasting. These activities will help prepare children to begin printing experiences with the letters of the alphabet (see page 42). Even though children find upper case letters easier to print than lower case letters, it is important that they be exposed to both. They should be given models and charts to follow so that they can correct and improve their own work. Since learning to print is a tedious task for young children, early printing experiences should be presented as informal, unstressful activities. Although the teacher should be alert to disability patterns (e.g., consistent letter reversals), she should not make an issue over the rightness or wrongness of early printing efforts.

Another way to train children toward independent writing is through oral dictation. Through group and individualized dictation sessions, children acquire an awareness of letter and word formation, grammar, and basic communication skills requisite to personal writing. As their teacher writes down and reads back dictation, children see and hear the structure and usage of language.

FEATHERS IN MY CAP

From this oral foundation, children usually want to experiment with independent writing. The teacher should be alert to these interests. She can provide opportunities for copy work using familiar words and sentences as beginning writing experiences. Children will progress in independent writing as they become confident and proficient in the skills required for a given task.

Activity 27: My First Dictionary

As a beginning writing experience, a teacher may want to have her children make a class dictionary composed of key words learned during the school year. Using words taken from the key word bank, the teacher helps her children sort and alphabetize the cards. To facilitate printing key words, she draws three horizintal lines on the left margin of each page and encourages children to print words over the lines. After each child has printed a key word, the teacher records the meaning and prints it next to the word. The dictionary can be illustrated and covered with a sturdy material that will withstand lots of busy little hands turning pages.

Activity 28: The Chatterbox

The teacher can designate a large corner of wall space "The Chatterbox," which is a place where children's news can be hung. She can outline the space with colored masking tape so that it has the appearance of a box. Children's dictation should be recorded by the teacher on large, lined paper (suggested size: 24" x 36"). Each day a child gets to "write" a news story containing four or five sentences. When the teacher has read the story back to the child, key words should be underlined and printed by the child in the language center.

Activity 29: The KK Corner

This is another way of introducing children to writing experience that is both fun and educational. Children take turns bringing a favorite recipe from home to contribute to a recipe corner located in a kitchen section of the housekeeping center or some other related activity area. The children may like to refer to this space as the "KK Corner" (Kindergarten Kitchen). When children bring in recipes from home, the teacher prints them on large lined paper asking children to sign their names and illustrate the recipes if they wish. During a read-aloud session, children can select key words that appear in their recipes such as *eggs, butter, flour, salt*. These words can be printed by the teacher on a chalkboard for children to copy during free activity time. Since this will be an ongoing activity and the same ingredients will be used over and over, children will feel comfortable and familiar with the sight words.

Activity 30: Rhyming Time

Another excellent way to introduce children to the fundamentals of various writing experiences is to set up a "rhyming time" center. On this section of a classroom wall, the teacher can have children dictate favorite finger plays, poems, and nursery rhymes. Included in this section should be children's original verse. The teacher can provide a first line, such as "There was an old woman from Bloat . . . " and have children provide a second line in rhyming verse. Children can illustrate original verses, select key sight words and practice printing these words in the language center. (Teachers should always try to dress up copy work papers with happy faces, doodles or stickers).

Activity 31: I Can Write!

Children should be encouraged to write short sentences containing key words and instant words. To prepare for this activity, the teacher prints four or five words on small index cards (e.g., bear, the, sad, is), and places them in random order in front of a child. After reading each word, the child must unscramble the words and put them into a sentence. When the child has read the entire sentence with the teacher, he can write it in a copy work notebook in the language center.

ART

Art is a natural and necessary form of communication in early childhood education. Young children are usually fascinated with the act of creating with their hands, shaping and reshaping until they are ready to move on to something else that sustains their curiosity. Often young children become absorbed in all mediums of art available in a classroom: working with clay or wood, finger painting, chalk drawings, collage, paper construction, stamping and printing, embroidery, and water color. The touch, the smell, and the visual appeal of creative expression cannot be surpassed on an experiential level for young children. No matter what the mood or persuasion, children always find time for art.

Activity 32: An Artist In Our Classroom

The teacher asks an artist friend to visit her classroom in order to introduce children to formal painting experiences on a real canvas. The artist begins her lesson by telling the children something about herself: why and what she likes to paint, how she feels she is communicating with paints, where and when she paints, etc. After demonstrating her techniques on a canvas, she provides an opportunity for children to paint on one also. When the children have finished applying paint to the surface of the canvas, the class can discuss the meaning of the painting as they perceive it. They may want to agree upon a title for their abstract masterpiece!

Activity 33: A Still Life

The teacher may like to show the class still life pictures, quiet pictures of stationary objects, painted by such artists as Paul Cezanne, Pablo Picasso, Georges Braque and Juan Gris. Discussing the elements of cubism, the teacher can demonstrate how an unusual arrangement of geometric shapes makes a delightful still life. The teacher creates a still life subject by placing interesting objects on a table for children to paint such as a guitar, a necktie, a newspaper, and a plate of oranges.

As they paint, children perceive shapes and color and begin to understand how placement can affect the appearance of an object (e.g., an orange blocking the full view of a necktie). Some children may even begin to sense a difference between foreground and background figures from a visual perspective.

Activity 34: Young Moderns!

Children can become modern artists under the influence of experts such as Jackson Pollock, Morris Louis or Pablo Picasso. The teacher explores various forms of modern art by showing copies of pictures by these famous artists and explaining how different approaches can create abstract art (e.g., splatter painting, stripes, and geometric shapes arranged in juxtaposition). The children can make a "modern art" portfolio using some of these techniques.

Drip paintings, drop paintings and splatter paintings require lots of room and some guidance from the teacher. Stripe paintings and geometric abstracts can be painted on a table or at the easel without assistance. Finger painting may also be incorporated into these art books.

Activity 35: Pop Art

The teacher introduces pop art to her children by describing some everyday objects that find their way into pop art. Stressing the ordinariness of the subjects and yet the uniqueness of their presentation in this form of artistic expression, she shows some pictures of important works of art and asks questions such as: "Why do you think Jasper Johns painted the American flag? Why do you think soup cans were interesting subjects for Andy Warhol? How can common items such as comic strips, household appliances, cosmetics and supermarket items be used in creative ways?" By combining classroom and home items, the children create their own pop art from labels from soup cans, saran wrap, tissue paper, numbers, comic strips, paper doilies, and cutouts from magazines.

Activity 36: Junk Art

Defining sculpture as the cutting, carving or shaping of material into a form that may or may not be recognizable to the viewer, the teacher suggests that children might like to create a "junk gallery" composed of assorted sculptures made from different materials. These items may be obtained in attics, basements, back yards, garages, scrap yards or city dumps. Parents should assist children in finding items that qualify as junk sculpture. To add to the gallery, children make their own sculpture from scraps of wood, wire, string and nails. The children may label their art work for display purposes.

Activity 37: Once Upon A Line

Many children like to experiment with various mediums of art in expressing themselves. Colored chalk can be messy but fun for young children. The tactile effect of chalk is especially pleasing to a child since it is light and easy to apply on a textured surface such as sandpaper.

In this project, a teacher can initiate a chalk drawing by making an interesting line on a piece of sandpaper. She suggests to a child that he "take the line for a walk" all over his sandpaper until the whole area is filled. When the child has finished his line drawing, he may like to experiment with a wet chalk picture using a variety of colored chalk dipped in water to bring out vivid linear patterns on sandpaper.

Activity 38: Light and Day

Children experience the influence of light on color through this activity. Painting with water color out-of-doors, the teacher initiates conversation by asking children what colors or hues they see around them; if they notice how colors change in the light as it drifts in and out of landscapes; how some colors make us feel differently than other colors. Before beginning their pictures, the children are directed to close their eyes and attempt to recreate the scene before them.

Activity 39: Guess What My Name Is Today

Children will love to add a paper mâché friend to the classroom roster. This friend will grow out of a thick mixture of flour and water, two large balloons, and strips of newspaper cut to approximately one-inch widths. The teacher begins the project by blowing up two balloons to serve as body molds for this paper mache creation. Children cover the balloons with several layers of the strips of paper moistened with a flour paste. When the two body parts dry, they can be glued together and painted. Large cardboard feet and ears may be added, and a tail if desired. As a personality emerges, the children may like to name this friend. They may even decide to change his name to correspond with the first sounds of letters (e.g., "Jumbo" for "J" day). A large name tag will help our friend be remembered by his many names.

CONCLUSION

The language experience program developed in this book was founded on the following child development principles: • children can learn to read at an early age through their natural abilities of communication if they are given the opportunity to experience themselves through creative expression; • language is nourished by acceptance, respect, and guidance; • children learn through experiences that permit exploration, discovery, and direct participation; • children must be given the opportunity to communicate these experiences in order to develop confidence and expand thinking processes and conceptual understandings; • reading is a skill that can incorporate virtually all facets of a child's growth and development.

If reading is approached through a building block process developed on a sound child-centered foundation, young children will begin their climb toward mastery and competency because the journey has become meaningful and important to them. Language experience provides a positive and secure foundation for children to move toward higher communication skills. As children begin to feel confident about their ability to communicate through language experiences, they will look upon beginning reading with as much enthusiasm as they put into their play world. Seeing themselves as primary participants in their own learning, young children will want to find out more about their potential and discover new ways to express themselves. Each step will naturally lead each child into progressive experiences and new accomplishments. With loving support and guidance, the young child will begin his climb and he will feel successful each step of the way.

"And Here I Am!"

... at the end, and the beginning of a language experience journey ...

Chapter 5

WORKSHEETS IN LANGUAGE EXPERIENCE ACTIVITIES

Worksheets 171

Key Words

Picture Story

172 FEATHERS IN MY CAP

Key Words

Picture Story

Worksheets

Key Words

Picture Story

174 FEATHERS IN MY CAP

Key Words

Picture Story

Worksheets 175

Key Words

Picture Story

176   FEATHERS IN MY CAP

Key Words

Picture Story

Worksheets 177

Key Words

Picture Story

178 FEATHERS IN MY CAP

Key Words

Picture Story

Key Words

Picture Story

FEATHERS IN MY CAP

Key Words

Picture Story

Worksheets   **181**

Key Words

Picture Story

182 FEATHERS IN MY CAP

Key Words

Picture Story

Worksheets 183

Key Words

Picture Story

184 FEATHERS IN MY CAP

Key Words

Picture Story

Key Words

Spring
Sun
Flower

Picture Story

186 FEATHERS IN MY CAP

Key Words

Picture Story

Worksheets **187**

Key Words

Picture Story

188 FEATHERS IN MY CAP

Key Words

Picture Story

Worksheets 189

Key Words

Picture Story

FEATHERS IN MY CAP

Key Words

Picture Story

Worksheets **191**

"This is my new pink umbrella. I don't want to get it wet."

FOOTNOTES

[1] See Roach Van Allen and Claryce Allen, *Language Experience in Reading* (Chicago: Encyclopedia Britannica Press, 1966); Doris M. Lee and Roach Van Allen, *Learning to Read Through Experience,* Second Edition, (New York: Appleton-Century-Crofts, Meredith Corporation, 1963); Roach Van Allen, *Language Experiences in Communication* (Boston: Houghton Mifflin Company, 1976); Russell G. Stauffer, *The Language-Experience Approach to the Teaching of Reading* (New York: Harper and Row, 1970); Mary Anne Hall, *Teaching Reading as a Language Experience* (Columbus, Ohio: Charles E. Merrill Publishing Co., 1976).

[2] Andrew Wilkinson, "Oracy and Reading," *Elementary English,* Vol. 51:8, 1974, p. 1103.

[3] Russell G. Stauffer, *The Language-Experience Approach to the Teaching of Reading* (New York: Harper and Row, 1970), pp. 268-275.

[4] Peter T. Pienaar, "Breakthrough in Beginning Reading: Language Experience Approach," *The Reading Teacher,* February 1977, pp. 489-496.

[5] See Roach Van Allen, *Language Experiences in Communication* (Boston: Houghton Mifflin Company, 1976).

[6] *Ibid.,* p. 120.

[7] Victor Lowenfeld, W.L. Brittain, *Creative and Mental Growth* (New York: Macmillan Publishing Co., 1975), pp. 3, 123.

[8] See Roach Van Allen and Claryce Allen, *Language Experience Activities* (Boston: Houghton Mifflin Co., 1976), pp. 51-140.

[9] See Carole Matthes, *How Children Are Taught To Read* (Lincoln, Nebraska: Professional Educators Publications, Inc., 1972).

[10] Roach Van Allen, *Language Experiences in Communication* (Boston: Houghton Mifflin Company, 1976), p. 217.

[11] Audrey Burie Kirchner, *Basic Beginnings* (Washington, D.C.: Acropolis Books, Ltd., 1979), pp. 124-125.

BIBLIOGRAPHY

Books

Allen, Roach Van. *Language Experiences in Communication.* Boston: Houghton Mifflin, 1976.

_____. *Language Experiences in Reading.* Chicago: Encyclopaedia Britannica Educational Corp., 1966, revised in 1972, Level I.

_____ and Allen, Claryce. *Language Experience Activities.* Boston: Houghton Mifflin, 1976.

_____. *Teacher's Resource Book: Language Experiences in Early Childhood.* Chicago: Encyclopaedia Britannica Educational Corp., 1969.

Burie, Audrey Ann and Heltshe, Mary Ann. *Reading With A Smile.* Washington, D.C.: Acropolis Books Ltd.

Cherry, Clare. *Creative Art For The Developing Child.* California: Fearon Publishers, 1972.

Croft, Doreen J. and Hess, Robert D. *An Activities Handbook for Teachers of Young Children.* Boston: Houghton Mifflin, 1972.

Dewey, John. *Experience and Education.* New York: Macmillan Company, 1963.

Fry, Edward. *Reading Instruction for Classroom and Clinic.* New York: McGraw-Hill, 1972.

Gaitskell, Charles. *Children and Their Art.* New York: Harcourt, Brace & World, 1958.

Ginott, Haim. *Teacher and Child.* New York: Macmillan company, 1972.

Glasser, William. *Schools Without Failure.* New York: Harper and Row, 1969.

Greene, Maxine. *Teacher As Stranger.* California: Wadsworth Publishing Co., 1973.

Grozinger, William. *Scribbling, Drawing, Painting: Early Forms of the Child's Pictorial Creativeness.* New York: Praeger, 1955.

Hall, Mary Anne. *Teaching Reading As A Language Experience.* Ohio: Charles E. Merrill Co., 1976.

Hildebrand, Verna. *Introduction To Early Childhood Education.* New York: Macmillan Company, 1971.

Hummel, Dean. *McDaniels, Carl.* How To Help Your Child Plan A Career. Washington, D.C.: Acropolis Books, Ltd., 1979.

Kellogg, Rhoda. *Analyzing Children's Art.* California: National Press Books, 1969.

Kirchner, Audrey Burie. *Basic Beginnings.* Washington, D.C.: Acropolis Books Ltd., 1979.

Lee, Doris M. and Allen, Roach Van. *Learning To Read Through Experience.* New York: Appleton-Century-Crofts, Meredith Corporation, 1963.

Leeper, Sarah H., Dales, Ruth J. Skipper, Dora S., and Witherspoon, Ralph L. *Good Schools for Young Children.* New York: Macmillan Company, 1968.

Lindberg, Lucile and Swedlow, Rita. *Early Childhood Education: A Guide For Observation and Participation.* New York: Allyn and Bacon, 1976.

Lowenfeld, Viktor. *Your Child and His Art:* Guide For Parents. New York: Macmillan Company, 1954.

_____ and Brittain, W. L. *Creative and Mental Growth.* New York: Macmillan Company, 1975.

Margrabe, Mary. *Media Magic.* Washington, D.C.: Acropolis Books Ltd., 1979.

Matthes, Carole. *How Children Are Taught to Read.* Nebraska: Professional Publication, Inc., 1972.

Merritt, Helen. *Guiding Free Expression in Children's Art.* New York: Holt, Rhinehart and Winston, 1966.

Miller, Mabel Evelyn. *Kindergarten Teacher's Activities Desk Book.* New York: Parker Publishing, 1974.

Platts, Mary E. *Launch: A Handbook of Early Learning Techniques for the Preschool and Kindergarten Teacher.* Michigan: Educational Service, 1972.

Rudolph, Marguerita, and Cohen, Dorothy H. *Kindergarten: A Year of Learning.* New York: Appleton-Century-Crofts, Meredith Corporation, 1964.

Sadker, Myra P. and Sadker, David M. *Now Upon A Time: A Contemporary View of Children's Literature.* New York: Harper and Row, 1977.

Spache, Evelyn B. *Reading Activities For Child Involvement.* Boston: Allyn and Bacon, 1976.

Spodek, Bernard. *Teaching In The Early Years.* New Jersey: Prentice-Hall, 1972.

Stant, Margaret A. *The Young Child: His Activities and Materials.* New Jersey: Prentice-Hall, 1972.

Stauffer, Russell G. *The Language Experience Approach to the Teaching of Reading.* New York: Harcourt, Brace and World, 1957.

Todd, Vivian E. and Heffernan, Helen. *The Years Before School.* New York: Macmillan Company, 1970.

Voight, Ralph. *The Learning Center Handbook.* Washington, D.C.: Acropolis Books Ltd., 1975.

Wills, Clarice D., and Lindberg, Lucile. *Kindergarten For Today's Children.* Chicago: Follett, 1967.

ANNOTATED BIBLIOGRAPHY FOR LEA

Brooks, Ron. *Timothy and Gramps,* New York: Bradbury Press, 1978. This is a tender and beautifully illustrated story about a shy and lonely little boy whose greatest pleasure is being with his grandfather. One day grandfather comes to school to share a special story with Timothy's classmates and things get better for Timothy, especially when he talks about grandfather.

Buckley, Helen. *Grandfather and I,* New York: Lothrop, 1959. Through sensitive and charming illustrations, this author captures a special feeling between grandfather and grandson—one of unhurried, relaxed time together—looking, listening, and learning about a little person's world.

Burningham, John. *Mr. Gumpy's Motor Car,* New York: Thomas Y. Crowell, 1973. Mr. Gumpy is everybody's friend because he is kind, patient, and always willing to oblige, especially when it comes to outings in his small, open car. There is usually a problem, like the day he packed his friends into the car and it began to rain. With everyone pushing, the car got out of the mud, and Mr. Gumpy promised another ride on another day.

ibid. *Mr. Gumpy's Outing,* New York: Holt, Rinehart & Winston, 1971. In this book, Mr. Gumpy takes his friends for a ride in his boat. Overloading his boat, Mr. Gumpy cautions everyone to be on best behavior. The boat tips over, but Mr. Gumpy's outing ends on a happy note with everyone enjoying tea together. Children will love the rhythmic pattern and repetition of the dialogue, and teachers can use the narrative sequencing of events to encourage comprehension and recall.

Burton, Virginia Lee. *The Little House,* Boston: Houghton Mifflin, 1943. Little house was very happy in the country but often wondered what it would be like to live in a busy city. When she became the victim of progress surrounded by grime and noise, the little house yearned for the country again. Rescued by caring people, she is carefully moved back to the country and loved again.

Carrick, Carol and Donald. *Sleep Out,* New York: Seabury Press, 1973. Christopher got a sleeping bag for his birthday and could hardly wait to sleep out all by himself. His back yard wasn't quite like the real woods, but Christopher and his dog, Bodger, finally got to experience the real thing during a summer vacation in the country. Christopher's camping out adventures will delight the young reader and provide a natural lead-in for language experience activities.

Feder, Paula Kurzband. *Where Does The Teacher Live?* New York: E.P. Dutton, 1979. Children are often curious about their teachers. Where do they live and what do they do besides teach? Nancy, Willy, and Alba are three little friends who decide to find out where their teacher, Mrs. Greengrass, lives. Guess what, she lives on a house boat on the 79th Street marina! All children will want to follow Mrs. Greengrass home.

Freeman, Don. *Corduroy.* New York: The Viking Press, 1968. Corduroy is a little teddy bear who lives in a big department store and longs for a real home. At last his opportunity comes when a little girl decides to purchase him with her own money, despite his somewhat tattered appearance. Corduroy's search to find the missing button on his pants will enthrall young children.

Freschet, Berniece. *The Happy Dromedary.* New York: Charles Scribner's Sons, 1977. It took a while for the dromedary to feel happy about herself and her unusual desire to make the desert her home. But with help from the animal king, she gradually became the proud and handsome animal she is today, walking across the golden desert — "plop-plop-plop."

Ginsburg, Mirra. *Mushroom In The Rain.* New York: The MacMillan Company, 1974. Children will listen with absolute attention as a mushroom grows to accommodate a mouse, a sparrow, a rabbit, an ant, and a butterfly seeking protection from the rain. But after all, that's what mushrooms do in the rain!

Haley, Gail E. *A Story, A Story.* New York: Atheneum, 1970. This is an African spider tale that tells about a defenseless man who succeeded against great odds to obtain Sky God's stories. Ananse's courage resulted in the surrender of a box of stories and the happiness of the villagers. Children will enjoy Ananse's quest, feats, and ultimate victory over Sky God.

Harper, Wilhelmina. *The Gunniwolf.* New York: E.P. Hutton, 1967. This is the delightful story of a little girl who doesn't heed her mother's warnings about venturing into the jungle near their little cottage. In search of flowers, the little girl moves happily into the jungle until she meets the fierce gunniwolf. In a rhythmic pattern of stopping, singing, and running, the little girl eventually finds her way back to the edge of the jungle and the safety of her home.

Hoban, Russell. *A Baby Sister For Frances.* New York: Harper and Row, 1964. Frances decides to run away when her new sister Gloria joins the family and receives too much attention. She packs her bag and runs away under the dining room table where she can hear her parents talk about how special she is and how they wish she would come home again. Frances doesn't stay away too long. Children with younger siblings will identify and sympathize with Frances.

Hutchins, Pat. *Happy Birthday, Sam.* New York: Greenwillow Books, 1978. Guess what! It's Sam's birthday, and he is a whole year older, ut he still can't reach the light switch, his clothes, the water tap, or the sink. . . . and worst of all, he can't even sail his new birthday boat. That is, until he opened grandpa's gift—a little chair just right for reaching things. Sam feels so big, now!

Isadora, Rachel. *Willaby.* New York: Macmillan Company, 1977. Willaby is a little girl who loves to draw and loves her teacher, Miss Finney. Sometimes making pictures can be a problem for Willaby like the time she forgot to sign her name to a get-well picture card for Miss Finney. During the week that Miss Finney was absent, Willaby was so upset that she drew thirty-seven get-well cards and signed her name to every one. Luckily, she didn't need to send them to Miss Finney, because she found a thank you note for her very first card. Miss Finney loves Willaby too!

Iwasaki, Chihiro. *The Birthday Wish.* New York: McGraw-Hill, 1972. Allison wishes that it will snow on her fifth birthday. Her happiness is interrupted by her friend's birthday party when Allison accidentally blows out the candles on Judy's cake. Allison feels upset for the rest of the day but wishes again for snow before going to sleep. The next day is a snowy day and Allison lets Judy blow out the candles on her fifth birthday cake. Children will want to discuss the many feelings that are suggested in this very special book.

Keats, Ezra. *The Snowy Day.* New York: The Viking Press, 1969. Peter revels in the specialness of a snowy day—crunchy tracks in the snow, snowmen, and angels. Peter loves snow so much that he decides to save a snowball in his warm house over night. The next morning his snowball is gone, but fresh snow has fallen. Children will love the colorful geometric figures contrasted by the whiteness of the snow and the magnificence of the moment for Peter.

ibid. *Whistle For Willie.* New York: The Viking Press, 1964. Everytime Peter puffed up his cheeks to whistle, nothing came out. How could a little dog take Peter seriously when he couldn't even whistle? Practice makes perfect, and Peter blew and blew until a whistle finally came out. Willie, his dog, just loved that whistle!

Lamorisee, Albert. *The Red Balloon.* New York: Doubleday & Company, 1956. This tender and symbolic story about a lonely little boy's love for a red balloon is a cherished contribution to children's literature. When neighborhood bullies taunt Pascal and throw stones at his beloved balloon, the sky is suddenly filled with balloons rising in freedom, carrying Pascal away from sadness and loneliness.

Lionni, Leo. *Alexander and the Wind-Up Mouse.* New York: Random House, 1969. This is the story about a real mouse and a wind-up mouse and their special friendship. Alexander thought he wanted to be a wind-up mouse like Willy until the day came when Willy was put in a throw away box with other old toys. Helped by a magical lizard and a purple pebble, Willy was turned into a real mouse to live happily ever after in Alexander's hole.

ibid. *Frederick*. New York: Random House, 1967. As other field mice busily gathered food for winter, Frederick gathered sun rays, colors, and conversation. When winter days dragged on and food became short, Frederick entertained his friends with warmth, color, and poetry.

ibid. *Tico And The Golden Wings*. New York: Random House, 1964. Tico is a little bird born without wings and dependent upon friends for survival. The day comes when Tico magically grows golden wings to the amazement and envy of other birds. Tico uses these wings as gifts for the poor and helpless until they are all gone and replaced by plain, black wings. Even with black wings, Tico is not an ordinary bird, for he understands the spirit of kindness and compassion.

McKloskey, Robert. *Make Way For Ducklings*. New York: The Viking Press, 1941. Mrs. Mallard was very particular about finding a suitable place to nest and raise her offspring, and Mr. Mallard was very patient with her. They finally settled on a quiet spot on the Charles River, and the little ducklings arrived just in time. As the ducks grew older, the Mallards decided to move to a livelier home in the public gardens where Michael, a friendly policeman, assisted them in living happily ever after.

Merriam, Eve. *Mommies At Work*. New York: Alfred A. Knopf, 1961. Children will experience mommies in a variety of roles; making cookies, kissing places that hurt and places that don't hurt, working on ranches, building bridges. But best of all, mommies come home to a lot of love at the end of the day. This is an excellent book for role identification in that women are viewed as mommies and career persons actively involved in a wide variety of jobs.

Miles, Miska. *Annie and the Old One.* Boston: Little, Brown, 1971. This sensitive book suggests that life and death are a part of a continuing process. Annie is a little Navajo girl who learns that when her mother finishes weaving a rug, it will be time for her beloved grandmother to die and return to the earth. Annie resists the inevitable death of her grandmother and tries to prevent the completion of the rug. When the old one explains that it is time for her to return to the earth, Annie understands and is filled with the wonder of it all.

Piper, Watty. *The Little Engine That Could.* New York: Platt & Munck, 1930. Children still love this classic because it appeals to their sense of curiosity, love for objects that they can identify with, and desire to make things right despite obstacles and shortcomings. The little blue engine huffs and puffs over the mountain with good things for little boys and girls because every little reader is saying, "I know you can!"

Schick, Eleanor. *One Summer Night.* New York: Wiliam Morrow & Co., 1977. On a warm, summer evening in a crowded corner of a city, Laura feels a soft wind and begins to dance. When neighbors hear the music, they stop what they are doing and begin to dance, too. Soon the whole street comes alive with gayety and friendship.

Scott, Ann Herbert. *On Mother's Lap.* New York: McGraw Hill, 1972. Michael is a little Eskimo boy who loves to sit on mother's big lap with reindeer blanket, boat, dolly, and puppy. Michael is not so generous about welcoming his baby sister to mother's lap, however. Mother shows Michael that her lap is big enough for one more and Michael is happy. The sense of intimacy and simple pleasure reflected in this book is very moving. Everyone will want to get on mother's lap!

ibid. *Sam.* New York: McGraw-Hill, 1967. Sam is the youngest member of a black family who feels that he is in the way because everything he tries to do is met with gentle "not nows" from family members. Mother soon realizes his feelings of rejection and isolation and finds something important for Sam to do. Siblings can identify with Sam's need to be needed and the unintentional "busy messages" that family members put forth to little ones.

Sendek, Maurice. *Where The Wild Things Are.* New York: Harper and Row, 1963. When Max is punished and sent to his room without dinner, he decides to sail away to the land of the wild things. While there he becomes the king of the wild things! When it is time for Max to return home, he sails back to his very own room—and his dinner is still hot. When children decide that the monsters are friendly, funny creatures, they want to join Max in his adventures.

Steig, William. *Amos and Boris.* New York: Farrer, Straus, Giroux, 1971. This is the story of trust and friendship between a little mouse and a huge whale. As each found ways to help the other survive in water and on land, Amos and Boris overcame barriers that might have separated them. In touching ways they communicated their needs, affection, and final farewell.

ibid. *Sylvester and the Magic Pepple.* New York: Simon and Schuster, 1969. This is the story of an endearing little donkey who uses a magic pebble to escape from a lion, only to find himself turned into a rock from which he cannot escape. Eventually, the donkey and his family are happily reunited in a tender scene.

Steptoe, John. *Stevie.* New York: Harper and Row, 1960. Through black dialect and vivid illustrations depicting a universal situation, this book describes feelings of a boy toward a little boy who comes to live in his house under his mother's care. Little Stevie disrupts Robert's life to the extent that Robert just wishes he would go away. When that day comes, however, Robert confesses affection for the little fellow, acknowledging that he is "sort of" like a brother.

Taylor, Mark. *Henry The Explorer.* New York: Atheneum: 1966. Henry and his little dog Angus loved to explore together. One day Henry's curiosity led him into a cave where he saw an image of a huge bear. Even worse, it was very dark when he started home and his mom was very worried about him. That night in the safety of his own bed, Henry and Angus planned their next outing.

Udry, Janice. *A Tree Is Nice.* New York: Harper and Row, 1956. Trees can do so many nice things. They can fill up the sky, make forests, provide havens for cats, and homes for birds. They can even shade cows and picnicers on hot summer days. This beautifully illustrated book will sensitize children to changing seasons and the importance of trees.

ibid. *What Mary Jo Shared.* Chicago: Albert Whitman & Co., 1966. Mary Jo needed to share with her classmates during show and tell but everything she thought of someone else had already shared. One day she invited her daddy to school and shared him in a sweet and comfortable way. Mary Jo and her friends delighted in the specialness of her first sharing.

Viorst, Judith. *The Tenth Good Thing About Barney.* New York: Atheneum, 1971. A little boy is very upset about the death of his cat, Barney, and the family decided to hold a funeral for their pet. They have no problem expressing nine good things about Barney, but they can't quite think of the tenth thing to say about the cat. When the father covers the ground with flower seeds, the little boy finds one more good thing to say. Barney will help the flowers grow! In this book, death is handled in a gentle and positive way that young children can relate to.

Waber, Bernard. *Ira Sleeps Over.* Boston: Houghton Mifflin, 1972. Ira is very attached to his teddy bear, Ta Ta, but to avoid looking babyish, he thinks it best to leave him home when he goes to his friend's house for a sleep over. Ira is not completely comfortable with this important decision and his sister doesn't make it any easier for him. Thankfully, his friend Reggie pulls out his teddy bear during a ghost story session and Ira rushes home for Ta Ta.

ibid. *You Look Ridiculous Said the Rhinoceros To The Hippopotamus.* Boston: Houghton Mifflin, 1966. A little hippopotamus is very insecure about her appearance. After all, she doesn't have a shell like a turtle, ears like an elephant, a horn like a rhinoceros, a tail like a monkey, a mane like a lion, spots like a leopard, or a voice like a nightingale. One day she dreamed that she looked like all her friends and she certainly didn't like what she saw. From then on, she was happy being a big, fat, wonderful hippopotamus.

Wolf, Bernard. *Tinker and the Medicine Man.* New York: Random House, 1973. Tinker is a Navajo Indian boy from Monument Valley, Arizona with an ambition to become a medicine man like his father and grandfather. He goes to school to learn English but spends his summers reliving ancestral traditions with his family. The writer uses photographs to depict Indian life and emphasize the continuity of common bonds despite the changing times.

Zolotov, Charlotte. *William's Doll.* New York: Harper and Row, 1972. William wants a doll of his very own, a wish that concerns his family. Grandmother understands the nature and importance of this need and buys William a doll. This book is helpful in freeing children from insensitive stereotyping.

FILM ADAPTATIONS

The film distributor for the followinging list of 16 mm. films is Weston Woods, Weston, Ct. 06880. Sound filmstrips, books, and records are also available for most of the films selected.

Andy and the Lion, 10 minutes, Caldecott Honor Book.

Beast of Monsieur Racine, 9 minutes, animated, first prize children's category, International Animation Film Festival.

Blueberries for Sale, 9 minutes, Caldecott Honor Book, ALA Notable Children's Book.

Caps for Sale, 5 minutes, ALA Notable Children's Book.

Changes, Changes, 6 minutes, animated, ALA Notable Children's Book.

Chicken Soup with Rice, 5 minutes, animated, ALA Notable Children's Book.

The Cow Who Fell in the Canal, 9 minutes.

Crow Boy, 13 minutes, Caldecott Honor Book, ALA Notable Children's Book.

Curious George Rides a Bike, 10 minutes.

Drummer Hoff, 6 minutes, animated,, Caldecott Honor Book, ALA Notable Children's Book.

Goggles, 6 minutes, Caldecott Honor Book.

The Happy Owls, 7 minutes, animated, ALA Notable Children's Book.

Harold and the Purple Crayon, 8 minutes, animated.

Harold's Fairy Tale, 8 minutes, animated, Grand Prize, Harrisburg Film Festival.

Hercules, 11 minutes.

In A Spring Garden, 6 minutes.

A Letter to Amy, 7 minutes.

The Little Drummer Boy, 7 minutes, ALA Notable Children's Book.

The Little Red Lighthouse, 9 minutes, ALA Notable Children's Book.

Make Way for Ducklings, 11 minutes, Caldecott Honor Book, ALA Notable Children's Book.

Mike Mulligan and His Steam Shovel, 11 minutes.

Patrick, 7 minutes, animated, Gold Medal at Atlanta International Film Festival.

Peter's Chair, 6 minutes.

Petunia, 10 minutes, animated.

A Picture for Harold's Room, 6 minutes, animated.

Rosie's Walk, 5 minutes, animated, Cine Golden Eagle Blue Ribbon, American Film Festival.

The Selfish Giant, 14 minutes, animated, German State Prize—Most Beautiful German Children's Film.

The Snowy Day, 6 minutes, animated, Caldecott Honor Book ALA Notable Children's Book, Best Children's Film, Venice Film Festival.

Stone Soup, 11 minutes, Caldecott Honor Book, ALA Notable Children's Book.

The Story About Ping, 10 minutes, Award of Merit, Columbus Film Festival.

A Story, A Story, 10 minutes, animated.

Strega Nonna, 9 minutes, animated, Caldecott Honor Book, ALA Notable Children's Book.

The Three Robbers, 6 minutes, animated, ALA Notable Children's Book.

Time of Wonder, 13 minutes, Caldecott Honor Book, ALA Notable Children's Book.

Where The Wild Things Are, 6 minutes, Caldecott Honor Book, ALA Notable Children's Book.

Whistle for Willie, 6 minutes, animated, ALA Notable Children's Book.

Rental Sources for Children's Films Cited:

Weston Woods
Weston, Ct. 06880

Center for Instructional Media and Technology
University of Connecticut, Film library
Stanford, Ct. 06268

Media Library, Audio-Visual Services
University of Iowa
Iowa City, Iowa, 52240

Boston University, School of Education
Krasker Memorial Film Library
Boston, Mass. 02215

Film Rental Center of Syracuse University
Syracuse, N.Y. 44240

Kent State University
Audio-Visual Services
Kent, Ohio 44242

Portland State University
Continuing Education Film Library
Portland, Oregon 97207

University of Utah
Educational Media Center
Salt Lake City, Utah 84112

Modern Film Rentals
2323 New Hyde Park Rd.
New Hyde Park, N.Y. 11040

CHILDREN'S RECORDS

CHILDREN'S LITERATURE: STORY TELLING ALBUMS

Alice in Wonderland, read by Joan Greenwood and Stanley Holloway, Caedmon.

Cinderella in Story and Songs, story and lyrics by Peter Haas, Pickwick International.

Curious George and Other Stories, read by Julie Harris, Caedmon.

Hansel and Gretel, with music from the opera by Humperdink, Disneyland.

The Little Engine That Could, Disneyland.

The Little Tailor, read by Peter Ustinov, Angel Recordings.

Madeline & Other Bemelmans, read by Carol Channing, Caedmon.

Mary Poppins, read by Maggie Smith and Robert Stephens, Caedmon.

The Nutcracker Suite, Dance of the Hours, Disneyland.

Petunia, read by Julie Harris, Caedmon.

Puss in Boots and Other Fairy Tales From Around the World, retold by Anabel Williams-Ellis, Caedmon.

Snow White and Other Fairy Tales, read by Claire Bloom, Caedmon.

The Story of Babar, read by Louis Jourdan, Caedmon.

The Tale of Peter Rabbit and Other Stories by Beatrix Potter, read by Claire Bloom, Caedmon.

The Tale of Squirrel Nutkin, read by Clair Bloom, Caedmon.

The Three Little Pigs, Disneyland.

The Ugly Duckling and Other Tales, read by Boris Karloff, Caedmon.

The Wind in The Willow, read by Jessica Tandy and Hume Cronyn, Pathways of Sound.

Winnie-the-Pooh, read and sung by Carol Channing, Caedmon.

The Wizard of Oz, Disneyland.

READ ALONG RECORDS AND BOOKS

Disneyland Records:
Bambi, Dumbo, The Little Red Hen, 101 Dalmations, The Ugly Duckling, The Little House, Sleeping Beauty, The Gingerbread Man, Pinocchio, How The Camel Lost His Hump, Peter Pan and Wendy.

RCA Records:
Dance-A-Story Records, Little Duck, Noah's Ark, Magic Mountain, Balloons, Brave Hunter, Flappy & Floppy, The Toy Tree, At The Beach.

Scott Foresman Talking Story Book Box:
Ask Mr. Bear, Brownie, Goggles, The Wild Duck & The Goose, M is for Moving, Just Me, Joey's Cat.

Weston Woods Books and Records:
See film selection, Appendix _____.

General Records:
Animals Songs and Stories, RCA; *Can't Help Singing,* RCA; *Creative Movement and Rhythmic Expression,* Hap Palmer, Educational Activities, Inc.; *Discussion Starters,* RCA; *Fantasyland Collection,* RCA; *Getting To Know Myself,* Hap Palmer Educational Activities, Inc.; *Great Children's Favorites,* Arthur Fiedler, RCA; *Ideas, Thoughts and Feelings,* Hap Palmer, Educational Activities, Inc.; *Sounds of Animals* (Farm and Zoo), Folkway Records; *You Read To Me, I'll Read To You,* John Ciardi, Pathways of Sound.

SCHOOL SUPPLY COMPANIES

Addison-Wesley Publishing Company
Jacob Way, Reading, Mass. 01867

Allyn and Bacon
470 Atlantic Avenue, Boston, Mass. 02210

Bemiss-Jason Corp.
3250 Ash Street, Palo Alto, Calif. 94306

Childcraft Education Corp.
20 Kilmar Road, Edison, N.J. 08817

Constructive Playthings
1040 E. 85th Street, Kansas City, MO. 64131

David C. Cook Publishing Company
850 North Grove Avenue, Elgin, Ill. 60120
(excellent resource for instructional pictures)

Denison's
9601 Newton Avenue South, Minneapolis, Minn. 55431

Disney Schoolhouse Products
500 South Buena Vista, Burbank, Calif. 91505

Edu-cards
380 Madison Avenue, N.Y., N.Y. 10017

Education Center
1042 Lindsay Street, Greensboro, N.C. 27405

Houghton Mifflin Co.
1 Beacon Street, Boston, Mass. 02107

Ideal School Supply Company
11000 Lavergne Avenue, Oak Lawn, Ill. 60435

Incentive Publications
P.O. Box 120189, Nashville, Tenn. 37212

Instructo-McGraw-Hill
Cedar Hollow & Matthews Rd., Paoli, Penna. 19301

Instructor Curriculum Materials,
Division of Instructor Publications,
7 Bank Street, Dansville, N.Y. 14437

Little Kenny Publications Inc.
1315 West Belmont Street, Chicago, Ill. 60657

Macmillian Arts & Crafts Company
9645 Gerwig Lane, Columbia, Md. 21046

Macmillan Publications
Front & Brown Streets, Riverside, N.J. 08370

Peck, Inc.
516 Lafayette Rd., St. Paul, Minn. 55101

Scott, Foresman & Co.
1900 E. Lake Avenue
Glenview, Ill. 60025

Trend Enterprises
300 9th Avenue, S.W., New Brighton, Minn. 55112
(excellent resource for visual aids, bulletin boards and instructional material).

SUBJECT INDEX

CHAPTER 1
A Language Experience Approach to Reading
What is LEA? 18-19
Research Validation 19-20
Language Development During The Early Years 20-21
Language Experience in Early Childhood Education 22
Art As Communication 22-25

CHAPTER 2
A Language Experience Model For Early Education
Group Interaction (Step 1) 29-33
   Child Centered Guidelines for Group Interaction 30-31
   How Often Should A Language Experience Theme Be Presented? 31-32
   How Does The Teacher Select Topics For Sharing Time? 32-33
Children's Art (Step 2) 33-37
   Procedure 33-36
   Materials 36
   Language Center 36-37
Recording (Step 3) 37-39
   Procedure 37-38
   Integrating Group Stories 38-39
Reading (Step 4) 39-45
   Procedure 39-40
   Integrating Early Reading Approaches with Step 4 41-45

    The Language Experience Sight Word Approach 41
    Letter Recognition 42
    Phonic Approach 42-43
    Instant Words 43-45
Summary 45-46
Language Experience Activity Themes 49-78
Patterns and Resources for Chapter II 79-85
High Frequency Word List 80
Upper and Lower Case Letter Chart 81-82
Sample Invitation 83
Diagram of a Language Center 84
Pattern: Feathers In My Cap 85

CHAPTER 3
Language Experience In The Classroom and In The Home

Establishing A Climate For Language Experience 88-92
    The Classroom Environment 88-89
    The Role of the Teacher 90-91
    The Home Environment 92
Activities 95-134
    Language Experience In The Classroom 95-118
    Language Experience In The Home 119-134

CHAPTER 4
Classroom Activities In The Language Arts

Integrating Language Arts Activities In The Classroom 138-168
    Reading 138-149
    Listening 150-155
    Speaking 156-159
    Writing 160-163
    Art 164-168
Conclusion 169-170
Worksheets in Language Experience Activities 171-191

TITLE INDEX

ACTIVITIES

Themes Based on Unit Studies
My Discovery Bag 51-52
Animal Friends 53-54
My Hands 55-56
My Mouth 59-60
Faces 61-62

Self Contained Themes
Indian Sand Painting 67-68
A Nature Walk 71-72
Circus Fun 73
Feathered Friends 77-80

Experience Themes: In The Classroom
Balloons 97-99
Big and Small 101-102
Families 105-106
"The President" 109-110
Thanksgiving 113-114
A Trip To The Firehouse 117-118

Experience Themes: In The Home
My Trouble Dolls 121
Gingerbread Friends 123-124
It's Snowing In My House 125
Dromedaries Weren't Always Happy 127-128
Boxes of Fun 131
Cindy the Caterpillar 133-134

Classroom Activities
Key Word Charts 139-141
Group Word Banks 142-143
Individual Word Banks 143-144
What Am I? 145
Tell A Tall Tale 145
A Tisket, A Tasket, A Key Word In Your Basket 146
Going Fishing 146
Call-A-Friend 147
The Terrible Troll 147
Toss and Read 148

To Market, To Market 148
The Reading Tree 149
A Trip To An Animal
    Farm 151
A Trip To A City 152
Country Sounds 152
Who Is Knocking At My
    Door? 153
Fly Pigeon, Fly 153
Baby Steps and Giant
    Steps 154
Listen To Mr. Gumpy 154
Colors On Parade 155
Show And Tell 156
A Pet Show 157
Hansels and Gretels 157
A Monkey's Tail 158

Phone A Friend 158-159
Puppet Pigs 159
My First Dictionary 161
The Chatterbox 161-162
The KK Corner 162
Rhyming Time 163
I Can Write! 163
An Artist In Our
    Classroom 164
A Still Life 165
Young Moderns! 165-166
Pop Art 166
Junk Art 167
Once Upon A Line! 167
Light and Day 168
Guess What My Name Is
    Today? 168

Additional Activities

Additional Activities

Additional Activities

Additional Activities

Additional Activities

Additional Activities

Additional Activities

Additional Activities

BRIGHT IDEAS!

for teachers

Easy, practical, fun games and activities to save you time and stimulate *all* your pupils

☐ **Reading with a Smile / 90 Reading Games that Work by Audrey Burie & Mary Heltshe**
Easy-to-make, child-tested, teacher-made games to stimulate an active interest in reading skills development
200 p., 5½ X 11, illustrated, index
ACEO-053-6, Grades Pre-K-6 **$8.95**

☐ **Science Fun Every Day in Every Way**
A Total Enrichment Calendar of Ideas and Activities for Every Year by Amy Benham and Doris Ensminger
in cooperation with the National Science Teachers Association
38 p., 11 X 17, Subject Index, Monthly Activity Index, Cross-referenced
ACEO-190-7, Grades K-8 **$9.50**

☐ **The Now Library Media Center**
A Stations Approach with Teaching Kit by Mary Margrabe
For each of 80 behavioral objectives, a teacher-made station and exercise sheets for developing media skills
162 p., 8½ X 11, reproducible stations Complete Teaching Kit, index
ACEO-213-X, Grades K-8 **$8.95**

☐ **Media Magic**
Games & Activities for the Gifted and the Not-So-Gifted by Mary Margrabe
More than 100 activities and easy-to-make games that make all media into learning tools for all disciplines.
148 p., 6 X 9, illustrated, index
ACEO-213-X, Grades K-8 **$7.95**

☐ **The Learning Center Idea Book by Ralph Claude Voight**
Ready-to-use, classroom-tested stations in all basic skill areas. Just tear them out and hang them up.
102 p., 12 X 18, illustrated, index
ACEO-399-3, Grades K-6 **$12.50**

☐ **Colonial Games 'n Fun Handbook by Adah Parker Strobell**
254 games, songs, dances, crafts, plays from America's past
174 p., 8 X 9, illustrated, index
ACEO-183-4, Grades K-8 **$6.95**

☐ **The Three R's**
A Handbook for Teachers, Tutors and Parents by Gary Don Hadley
The complete classroom-tested instructional manual for teaching the basics in the classroom . . . or in the home.
266 p., 6 X 9, Reading Vowel Lists, Arithmetic Practice Pages, Use of TV to Supplement Regular 3R's Instructional Program, index
ACEO-186-9, Grades K-8 (remedial) **$5.95**

☐ **303 Mini-Lessons for Social Studies by Mary Ann Williamson**
A new approach to social studies which teaches skills through classroom-tested activities geared to age level.
154 p., 8 X 9, illustrated, index
ACEO-037-4, Grades K-12 **$6.95**

☐ **Basic Beginnings**
A Handbook of Learning Games by Audrey Burie Kirchner
(author of Reading with a Smile)
A complete program design for introducing Pre-K-2 pupils to basic skills with learning environment plans, daily schedules, individualized instruction techniques, plus
 *50 imaginative reproducible games in reading and math readiness, visual perception, sequence/classification
 *20 language arts activities in make-believe, sensory and self experiences
 *9 themes for study in social studies, science and literature
 *lesson plans and 23 reproducible game patterns, 158 illustrations
240 p., 8½ X 11, 158 illustrations, index
ACEO-229-6, Grades Pre-K-2 **$12.95**

Order today!
Send check or charge to
☐ AmExp ☐ VISA ☐ MstChg
Acct. # _____
Exp. date _____
or Official P.O. # _____
(Please add $1.50 for postage & handling)
Name _____
Address _____
City _____ State ____ Zip ____

A Acropolis Books, Suite C
2400 17th St., N.W.
Washington, D.C. 20009